SKATING

BOY SCOUTS OF AMERICA
IRVING, TEXAS

Note to the Counselor

Skating activities present inherent safety concerns, primarily the risk of falls and collisions. The guidelines below emphasize prevention and are meant to cover all BSA skating programs. Scouts should always practice safety and courtesy and obey all local and rink or park rules. Every Skating merit badge program or activity must follow the BSA guidelines, which are set forth in the *Guide to Safe Scouting* and are repeated here. Review these guidelines with the Scout, and be sure that he understands each one.

1. BSA skating at any level shall be supervised by an adult at least 21 years of age, experienced in the use of skates and skateboards, willing to conscientiously accept responsibility for the safety of all participants, and committed to compliance with BSA safety guidelines and local laws.

2. In-line skating, hockey, racing, or similar activities are to be held only in areas free of pedestrian and vehicular traffic, and hazardous fixed objects. No skating activity is authorized on streets that have not been blocked off to traffic.

3. Pathways and skating surfaces must be free of defects or features unsuited to skating. Evaluation of the area by the supervisor should precede any BSA activities.

4. Before permitting equipment to be used in a BSA activity, the supervisor should determine that all skates and skateboards are well maintained and in good repair consistent with the manufacturer's recommendations. Actual maintenance and repair are the responsibility of the owner.

5. For all street or pavement skating activities, participants should wear properly fitted helmets that meet American National Standards Institute (ANSI) standards; padded gloves; wrist supports; and elbow and knee pads. No street or pavement skating is authorized without helmets.

6. Skaters must *NEVER* "hitch a ride" on any vehicle.

7. Parents or legal guardians must be informed and must consent to youth participation in a BSA skating activity.

8. The adult supervisor must be sure that all participants understand and agree that skating is allowed only with proper supervision and in compliance with the safety guidelines. Youth members should respect and follow all directions and rules of the adult supervisor. When people know the reasons for rules and procedures, they are more likely to follow them. Supervisors should be strict and fair, showing no favoritism.

Skating merit badge instruction should follow the requirements, procedures, and techniques presented in this pamphlet for the discipline of choice (ice skating, roller skating, or in-line skating). The information contained in this pamphlet has been organized for the individual skating disciplines in a sequence that the authors have found to be most practical when working with Scouts. The learning objectives, which can be attained by the average Boy Scout, should emphasize safety and basic skill proficiency.

Requirements

1. Show that you know first aid for injuries or illnesses that may occur while skating, including hypothermia, frostbite, lacerations, abrasions, fractures, sprains and strains, blisters, heat reactions, shock, and cardiac arrest.

2. Complete ALL of the requirements for ONE of the following options.

ICE SKATING

    a. Do the following:

        (1) Give general safety and courtesy rules for rink skating. Discuss precautions that must be taken when skating outdoors on natural ice. Explain how to make an ice rescue.

        (2) Discuss the parts and functions of the different types of ice skates.

        (3) Describe the proper way to carry ice skates.

        (4) Describe daily skate care when skates are in use.

        (5) Describe how to store skates for long periods of time, such as seasonal storage.

    b. Do the following:

        (1) Skate forward at least 40 feet and come to a complete stop. Use either a two-footed snowplow stop or a one-footed snowplow stop.

        (2) After skating forward, glide forward on two feet, then on one foot, first right and then left.

        (3) Starting from a T position, stroke forward around the test area, avoiding the use of toe points if wearing figure skates.

    c. Do the following:

        (1) Glide backward on two feet for at least 25 feet.

        (2) Skate backward for at least 40 feet on two skates.

        (3) After gaining forward speed, glide forward on two feet, making a turn of 180 degrees around a cone, first to the right and then to the left.

d. Do the following:

    (1) Perform a forward shoot-the-duck until you're nearly stopped. Rise while still on one foot.

    (2) Perform forward crossovers in a figure eight pattern.

    (3) Take part in a relay race.

    (4) Perform a hockey stop.

ROLLER SKATING

a. Do the following:

    (1) Give general safety and etiquette rules for roller skating.

    (2) Discuss the parts and functions of the roller skate.

    (3) Describe five essential steps to good skate care.

b. Do the following:

    (1) Skate forward with smooth, linked strokes on two feet for at least 100 feet in both directions around the rink and demonstrate proper techniques for stopping.

    (2) Skate forward and glide at least 15 feet on one skate, then on the other skate.

c. Do the following:

    (1) Perform the crosscut.

    (2) Skate backward for at least 40 feet on two skates, then for at least 15 feet on one skate.

    (3) Skate forward in a slalom pattern for at least 40 feet on two skates, then for at least 20 feet on one skate.

    (4) Skate backward in a slalom pattern for at least 15 feet on two skates.

d. Do the following:

    (1) Shuttle skate once around the rink, bending twice along the way without stopping.

    (2) Perform a widespread eagle.

    (3) Perform a mohawk.

    (4) Perform a series of two consecutive spins on skates, OR hop, skip, and jump on skates for at least 10 feet.

  e. Do the following:

    (1) Race on a speed track, demonstrating proper technique in starting, cornering, passing, and pacing.

    (2) Perform the limbo under a pole placed at least chest-high OR shoot-the-duck under a waist-high pole and rise while still on one foot.

    (3) Perform the stepover.

    (4) While skating, dribble a basketball the length of the floor, then return to your starting position, OR push a hockey ball with a stick around the entire rink in both directions.

IN-LINE SKATING

  a. Do the following:

    (1) Give general and in-line skating safety rules and etiquette.

    (2) Describe the parts and functions of the in-line skate.

    (3) Describe the required and recommended safety equipment.

    (4) Describe four essential steps to good skate care.

  b. Do the following:

    (1) Skate forward with smooth, linked strokes on two feet for at least 100 feet.

    (2) Skate forward and glide at least 15 feet on one skate, then on the other skate.

    (3) Stop on command on flat pavement using the heel brake.

  c. Do the following:

    (1) Perform the forward crossover.

    (2) Perform a series of forward, linked swizzles for at least 40 feet.

    (3) Skate backward for at least 40 feet in a series of linked, backward swizzles.

    (4) From a strong pace, perform a lunge turn around an object predetermined by your counselor.

    (5) Perform a mohawk.

d. Do the following:

   (1) Perform a series of at least four one-footed downhill slaloms on pavement with a gentle slope.

   (2) Describe how to pass a pedestrian or another skater from behind.

   (3) Describe at least three ways to avoid an unforeseen obstacle while skating.

   (4) Describe two ways to get on and off a curb, and demonstrate at least one of these methods.

35006A
ISBN 0-8395-5006-5
©1999 Boy Scouts of America
1999 Edition

Contents

Introduction

Skating for Fun and Skill

This merit badge will introduce you to the exciting world of ice skating, roller skating, and in-line skating. Get ready for fun, challenges, and growing confidence in your skating abilities!

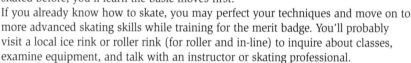

You'll choose either ice, roller, or in-line skating for this merit badge. If you haven't skated before, you'll learn the basic moves first. If you already know how to skate, you may perfect your techniques and move on to more advanced skating skills while training for the merit badge. You'll probably visit a local ice rink or roller rink (for roller and in-line) to inquire about classes, examine equipment, and talk with an instructor or skating professional.

Each kind of skating offers many possibilities beyond what you learn for the merit badge. For instance, both ice skating and roller skating include figure skating, freestyle, pairs, dance, hockey, and speed skating. In-line skating includes marathons, speed skating, hockey, and aggressive skating—street and vert.

There are many careers in skating. Besides skaters, the world of skating needs professional referees, examiners, judges, officials, coaches, and administrators. You'll find more information on skating at the end of this pamphlet, in the Skating Resources section.

Brief History of Skating

Early Ice Skating

Although it is not known exactly when skating began, scientists have evidence to support the theory that ice skating started in northern Europe well before the Christian era began. The first skate runners were made of bone. Later, they were constructed of wood. The wooden skate with a facing of iron first appeared in the 1300s.

Literature and painting reveal that ice skating was popular throughout the Middle Ages. King Harold of Norway (1035) was an ardent skater. In early times, skaters pushed themselves over the ice by using poles with picks in the tips.

History books refer to ice skating, too. When the Dutch fleet was frozen in the ice at Amsterdam in 1572, the Dutch repelled an attack by Spaniards after issuing ice skates to the defending musketeers. Marie Antoinette was a skater. Napoleon Bonaparte was rescued from drowning in 1791 after he fell through the ice while skating. Early American colonists described how Indians used ice skates to hunt muskrat.

The earliest form of skating competition was racing on ice skates. Speed skating records date from the 1700s, but it was not until 1885 that official events were held. Modern ice hockey began in Ontario, Canada, in 1855, but a 1670 Dutch painting shows a skater carrying a crude hockey stick while a ball lay on the ice nearby.

Skating has its own patron saint, St. Lidwina. An early woodcut shows the young saint lying by the bank of a river in Holland after she was injured in an ice skating accident in 1396.

Early Roller Skating

Roller skating originated in Holland in the early 1700s, as a natural all-season outgrowth of ice skating. Modeled after ice skates, the roller skates ran on wooden spools arranged in a row.

In 1760, Joseph Merlin, a Belgian musical-instrument maker and mechanic, was the first to make a pair of roller skates with metal wheels. In the following years, others tried to improve skate design.

When composer Giacomo Meyerbeer presented his opera *Le Prophete* in Paris in 1849, he included an ice skating scene in the third act. Meyerbeer needed to simulate ice skating by using skates devised for a wooden stage. He consulted M. Legrange, a machinist, who produced a skate that ran on iron wheels. The opera's "Ballet des Patineurs" (The Skaters' Ballet) amazed and delighted the audience. The opera was a success, and the public became greatly interested in roller skating.

All these early roller skates, with wheels in a line, were difficult to turn and stop.

Wheels and Blades

Around the time of the American Civil War, two innovations changed skating forever—the invention of the modern roller skate and the invention of refrigerated ice.

Plimpton roller skate

James L. Plimpton, an American, invented his "rocking" roller skate in 1863 so he could skate during the summer months. The skate had four wheels—two side-by-side in the front, and two in back. This arrangement allowed a skater to turn by leaning to one side or the other. Plimpton organized the New York Roller Skating Association and built a rink in New York City to accommodate his hobby. The rink became an instant success among high society. In the 1880s, new ball-bearing skates gave a smoother ride.

In 1850 an American physician, John Gorrie, patented a method for producing refrigerated ice. His invention later led to indoor rinks for year-round ice skating. The first indoor rink, called the Glaciarium, opened in London in 1875. The Palais de Glace, a circular rink, opened in Paris soon afterward. Before long a small number of indoor rinks were operating in locations around the world. Even sparsely populated Australia sported an ice rink.

Famous skaters have played important roles in the development of the sport of skating. Jackson Haines, an American ballet dancer who mastered ice skating, created new ideas in freedom of movement, interpretation, and dance on skates. He went to Europe in 1864 and gave exhibitions that created a sensation. Haines performed on roller skates as well, giving exhibitions of *Le Prophete* in several European cities. He is known as the "father of skating," and his graceful, free skating evolved into what is now known as the International Freestyle.

Figure skating became an Olympic event in 1908. In the late 1920s a Norwegian teenager named Sonja Henie revolutionized the sport. The first woman to wear white skates, she abandoned the restrictive female skating attire of the period and wore shorter costumes that shocked judges, contestants, and spectators. She won 10 world championships and three consecutive Olympic gold medals.

In the late 1930s Henie made a series of smash-hit ice-skating movies in Hollywood. Her movies stimulated an international interest and enthusiasm for ice skating that continues to grow. She toured the United States, Canada, and Europe with her own ice shows. Today the ice show is a form of entertainment enjoyed by many people throughout the world.

Associations, Competitions, and Tests

The sport of amateur figure skating in the United States was founded in 1921 by the United States Figure Skating Association. Amateur hockey is governed by the Amateur Hockey Association of the United States.

The Ice Skating Institute of America offers graduated tests for all skill levels in every area of skating, from the basic skills through figures, freestyle, pairs skating, ice dancing, hockey, and speed skating. These competitions are open to any amateur ice skater and include such events as precision and drill team competitions, trios, quartets, shadow skating, pairs similar (involving two males or two females), and skating acts.

Ice skating has grown in popularity, and ice hockey has grown at an extraordinary rate. Thousands of hockey clubs exist in the United States and Canada. Figure skating competitions are often televised, and both figure skating and speed skating are exciting parts of the Winter Olympic Games. The Olympics added speed skating for men in 1924 and for women in 1960.

Roller Competitions

A group of independent roller rink owners organized a skating association called the Roller Skating Rink Operators Association of America in 1937. This group, now known as the Roller Skating Association, encouraged the growth of roller skating both as sport and as recreation.

The association sponsored the first United States roller-skating championships in speed skating in 1937 and then added competition in figures and dance in 1939. World championships, sponsored by Federation Internationale de Roller Skating, involve competitors from Europe, North America, South America, Africa, Asia, and Australia.

In-Line Skating

Though the earliest roller skates had wheels in a line, the later side-by-side arrangement became the standard skate. Still, skate designers came up with new in-line designs now and then, but they didn't catch on.

Around 1980, brothers Scott and Brennan Olson, ice hockey players from Minnesota, modified an existing in-line skate so they and their friends could continue training in off-season. They added better wheels and a brake, and started manufacturing skates. When they sold their business to a larger company, marketing took off.

The sport experienced an explosion in growth when in-line skate manufacturers marketed the skate to trendy beach areas of southern California. By 1996, there were an estimated 27.5 million in-line skaters in the United States. In-line skating is one of the fastest growing sports in the United States; participation has increased nearly 800 percent from 1989 to 1996. This sport has attracted more participants than soccer, baseball, tennis, or football.

The International In-line Skating Association promotes safety and has an instructor certification program for three levels of skating.

Diet and Exercise

To be a champion you must eat well, exercise, and get the sleep you need. If you neglect any of these, you'll delay your progress as a skater.

Your objective should be to get proper nutrition, including vitamins and minerals, from a balanced diet, in order to produce the strength and stamina your daily practice sessions require. Study a copy of the Food Pyramid, published by the United States Department of Agriculture. It explains the number of recommended servings per day from different food groups. Follow a healthful schedule of meals and snacks. Your physician may have dietary advice for you, or a county extension office may recommend booklets on good dietary habits.

The next essential in your training program is good sleeping habits. Added to high-quality, regular meals, this will keep your body in excellent condition. Lack of sleep from keeping late hours will soon cause fatigue, and you'll tire after only a few minutes of skating practice. The amount of sleep you should have depends on your individual needs, but eight hours seems to be the norm.

A regular practice schedule usually allows you plenty of exercise, but there are other body-building exercises you can do, depending on the kind of skating you enjoy. For instance, weight lifting would be good for a pairs or fours team to strengthen arms and shoulders. Speed-skaters often take up cycling. A good all-around body-building exercise is swimming, which uses more muscles at the same time than any other activity. Many figure skaters have entered racing with the intent of building up their speed and stamina.

Emotional control is another necessary ingredient for successful skating—and for successful living. If you get plenty of sleep, have a healthful diet, avoid stress, noise, and health-destroying habits such as smoking, you will be a poised, prepared athlete—a potential champion.

First Aid

Like most sports, skating—whether on wheels or blades—has a unique set of risks and precautions. The conditions described here represent those for which any safety conscious skater should be prepared.

Hypothermia occurs when the body's core temperature falls below the normal range. Any combination of cool weather, wet skin or clothes, wind, exhaustion, or hunger can lead to hypothermia. Skating may present hypothermia risks. As the body cools, the victim will shiver in an attempt to create heat. Be aware of these danger signs: loss of muscle strength and coordination, as well as disorientation or incoherence, and pale or bluish skin tone. In severe stages, shivering stops, unconsciousness follows, and death is possible unless immediate treatment is received. Anyone who starts to shiver, or who shows discoloration around the lips or cheeks, should immediately be taken out of the activity and moved to a warm place. Any wet clothing should be removed and the victim should be thoroughly dried. If no warm shelter or other heat source is available, the victim should be pressed closely with one or more persons so that heat can be transferred through direct skin contact.

Heat reactions result from overheating when the body can't keep itself cool enough. If a skater feels dizzy, faint, nauseous, or weak; develops a headache or muscle cramps; or looks pale and is sweating heavily, treat for heat exhaustion.

- Have the person lie down in a cool, shady spot with feet raised.
- Loosen clothing and cool the person with a damp cloth or a fan.
- Have the victim sip water.

Recovery should be rapid. If the condition worsens, get medical help. **Heat-stroke** is the extreme stage where **dehydration** (body water loss) has caused a very high body temperature and a cessation of sweating. The pulse is extremely rapid and the person will be disoriented or unconscious. The victim must be cooled immediately through immersion or with cold packs, and the fluid level of the body must be increased. Treat for shock and seek emergency medical help.

Fractures are broken bones, injuries all too frequently associated with skating. There are two kinds: closed (simple) and open (compound). A closed fracture is a broken bone where the skin is not torn or punctured. If there is a wound through the skin at the break, it is called an open fracture.

Signs of a fracture may include

- Tenderness to the touch
- Swelling and discoloration
- Unusual or abnormal position or movement
- Grating sound or feeling
- Immobility
- Sharp snap sound or feeling at the time of the injury

Treatment includes keeping the victim still and quiet with no movement of the injured area. Treat for shock, if indicated. Apply cold packs to reduce pain and swelling. For open fractures, use direct pressure to control bleeding. In all cases, get medical help to the victim. If the victim must be moved, splint the fracture prior to transport. Improvised splinting procedures are discussed and illustrated in the *First Aid* merit badge pamphlet.

Sprains are caused by twisting, wrenching, or lifting movements that tear or stretch tissues around a joint. Such an injury causes sudden pain and swelling at the joint. There may be some discoloration, and the joint will likely be tender to the touch and very painful when moved. Sprains are relatively common injuries from skating falls. Elevate the injured joint, apply cold compresses, and treat as a fracture or broken bone.

The term **strain** usually refers to a less severe joint or muscle injury where tissues are not torn but may have been overextended or overstressed. Depending on the severity, treat the same as a sprain.

When a person is injured or under great stress, the circulatory system may fail to provide enough blood to all parts of the body. This condition is called **shock,** and it may accompany any serious skating injury. In severe cases it may be fatal. Indications include pale, moist, clammy or cool skin; weak and rapid pulse; weakness; shivering; thirst; nausea; or shallow, rapid breathing. Because of the risks and uncertainties that may accompany a serious injury, every victim should be treated for shock.

- Keep the victim lying down with the feet slightly elevated.
- Prevent loss of body heat.
- Keep the airway open and give rescue breathing if needed.
- If the victim is conscious, give water.
- Treat the underlying injury and get medical help.

Contusion is the medical term for bruises—like those black-and-blue marks that may appear on the arms and legs. Most bruises are not serious and are easy to recognize and treat. The discoloration is caused by blood leaking into damaged skin tissue, usually by a blow from a blunt object. Covering the site of a new bruise with a cold compress or towel for 30 minutes will help reduce discoloration, pain, and swelling. Also, slow the flow of blood into the damaged tissues by resting the injured area. To help fade the discoloration and reduce swelling, apply a warm, damp cloth 12 to 24 hours after the injury.

Bruises that include possible bone injury, or any contusions on the head or abdomen coupled with sharp or persistent pain, should be seen by a medical professional.

Lacerations, incisions, and **abrasions** (cuts and scrapes) may occur while skating, or more likely when falls occur on rough surfaces. As in other situations, the wound should be cleaned, disinfected, and covered. The unit or patrol first-aid kit should provide for minor wound treatment. For severe bleeding injuries, control bleeding with direct pressure or at pressure points until emergency medical help is available.

In skating, **blisters** are most likely to occur on the feet, and skaters should be attentive to any tenderness or sensitive areas ("hot spots") that indicate the start of a blister. You may be able to adjust lacing or socks to avoid friction on the sensitive area. If not, be smart: Listen to your body and quit for the day. If you have no choice to continue the activity, follow preventive steps such as taping and the use of commercial skin tougheners. Treat blisters when they do occur as in any other situation.

Frostbite may occur whenever flesh is exposed to low temperatures. Toes, fingers, nose, cheeks, and ears are especially susceptible. Skating in cold, windy weather risks frostbite if feet, hands, and face are not well-protected. Also, the body must be warm enough to supply warm blood to those areas susceptible to frostbite, so it is important to have warm clothing and cover for the head and torso as well as the extremities. As the flesh begins to freeze it reddens and is painful. In severe frostbite the skin stiffens and is grayish or whitish. Blisters may appear.

When frostbite occurs, immediately warm the affected area. Breathing on fingertips or placing chilled fingers beneath clothing and against warm skin, such as under the arms, is usually sufficient in mild cases. For more severe freezing, immerse the cold area in tepid or lukewarm (104 to 108 degrees F) water. Avoid heat or abrasion, which can injure or seriously damage tissue made sensitive by the cold. Blistering in severe cases requires sterile dressing, treatment for shock, and immediate medical attention.

Cardiopulmonary resuscitation (CPR) is the important first response in the event of a cardiac emergency, which may result from accidents where severe impact or other circumstances have caused respiratory and cardiac arrest. Persons trained in CPR should be included in every skating outing. The *Boy Scout Handbook* and the *First Aid* merit badge pamphlet explain these skills and when they should be used.

POWER ICE SKATING

Tips for the Beginner

Skates That Fit

When you visit an ice skating rink for the first time, you may have to rent skates. Rental skates are not sized like regular street shoes. Make sure you know your street shoe size and then, when renting skates, ask for one size smaller. (If you have a small foot, ask for a half-size smaller.) Your toes should come to the end of the skating boot but should not feel cramped. Try on the rental skates. If there is too much toe space, ask for a smaller size. Care and patience at skate-fitting time will help you skate far more effectively.

Before putting on your skates, make sure the laces are loosened all the way down; otherwise you may think the boot is too small when your foot is restricted just by the laces. With your foot correctly in place, pull up your socks to remove wrinkles. Pull the long tongue up firmly, in case you have pushed part of it down in front of your toes.

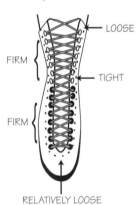

LOOSE

FIRM

TIGHT

FIRM

RELATIVELY LOOSE

When lacing your boots, don't overtighten near the toes. They should be free to wiggle. Lace firmly from the bottom of the boot until you reach the ankle area. On most boots, this area coincides with the top pair of eyelets. Above this area, most boots are equipped with hooks. At this point, lace tightly. The bottom hooks should be tightly laced, and then you may go back to lacing just firmly again. At the top, the lacing should be relatively loose or you will restrict circulation. Tuck in your laces.

Never attempt to learn to ice skate on skates that don't fit properly. A correct fit is essential. Also, although beginners don't need to have extremely sharp skates, the blades should not be blunt. To test for sharpness, run the back of your thumbnail across the edge of the blade with light pressure. An adequately sharpened edge should scuff off a fraction of thumbnail surface.

Many rinks offer renters a choice between hockey, figure, or speed skates. Figure skates are easier to learn on because they provide better ankle support. You can easily transfer to other types of skates later.

Understand the Edges

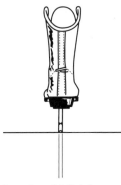

Take a look at the bottom of your figure skate blade. It has a concave groove running along its length. When you place the blade on the ice in an upright position, the two sharpened edges make contact with the ice. When the skate moves over the ice with both edges making contact, the skate will move in a straight line.

Now hold the skate upright on a smooth flat surface. Look at it from the side. You'll notice the blade is rockered (slightly curved), so only about an inch of its length is actually in contact with the surface. The rest of the blade does not touch. It's this degree of rockering that makes the figure skate maneuverable, permitting spins on one foot, just as a quarter will spin if you hold it vertically on a surface and flick it.

If the blade of a figure skate is touching the ice at an angle, only one of the two sharpened edges will cut into the ice, while the other edge will not make contact. Since the sharpened edge that is in contact is curved (rock-ered), the skate will move over the ice in a curving arc.

The direction the curve takes on the ice depends on

1. Which foot the skater is on

2. Which of the two edges of the skate is in contact with the ice

3. Whether the skater is going forward or backward

Skate edges have different names. As you look down at the skates you're wearing:

- The edge to the outside of the right foot blade is the **right outside edge**.
- The edge to the inside of the right foot blade is the **right inside edge**.
- The edge to the outside of the left foot blade is the **left outside edge**.
- The edge to the inside of the left foot blade is the **left inside edge**.

Knowing these terms will help you understand the different uses of edges as you learn skating skills.

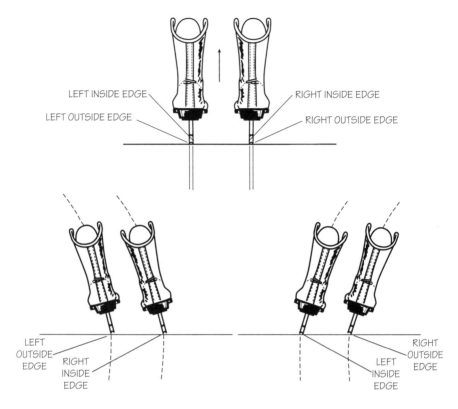

LEFT INSIDE EDGE
LEFT OUTSIDE EDGE
RIGHT INSIDE EDGE
RIGHT OUTSIDE EDGE

LEFT OUTSIDE EDGE
RIGHT INSIDE EDGE

RIGHT OUTSIDE EDGE
LEFT INSIDE EDGE

Once you understand the effects of the edges, you'll know that to make a curve to the **left** while skating forward, you must have your left outside edge or your right inside edge—or both of them—cutting into the ice.

To make a curving movement to the **right** while skating forward, you must have your right outside edge or your left inside edge—or both of them—cutting into the ice.

The Skating Leg and the Free Leg

The leg you're skating on is called the **skating leg,** while the leg that is removed from contact with the ice is termed the **free leg.** We also refer to the skating foot and the skating hip, as opposed to the free foot and the free hip.

As a general rule, the skating leg should be held in a flexed position, bending as the foot makes contact with the ice, and the free leg should be stretched as it leaves the ice. "While the skating leg bends, the free leg extends."

Safety

Rules and Etiquette

Learn and comply with the rink's safety and courtesy rules. The rules are designed to help prevent accidents and to make skating enjoyable for everyone.

Never eat, drink, or take food or beverages onto the ice. Never drop anything onto the ice where it could cause another skater to trip. If you do drop something onto the ice, remove it immediately. Do not chew gum.

If you fall, get up quickly, avoiding touching the ice with your hands as much as possible. Serious accidents while skating are rare, but most accidents involve cut fingers.

If you find yourself about to fall, don't grab onto another skater. Instead, try to lower your arms and bend your knees. This lowers your center of gravity. Try to remain on two feet. If you fall backward, keep your hands and fingers facing forward as they make contact with the ice.

Make sure you're adequately and warmly dressed. For figure skating, wear thin woolen socks. Wear gloves when you first learn to skate, but avoid scarves or hats.

Be sure you review and learn the BSA skating guidelines that appear in "Note to Counselor" at the beginning of this book.

Safety Rules at Ice Rinks

Ice skate blades should be used responsibly, like any other type of blade. Use blade guards when carrying your skates.

Ice rinks post their safety rules on notice boards. Rules may include:

- No eating or drinking on the ice.
- No playing of tag, follow-the-leader, or crack-the-whip.
- No cutting across the path of other skaters.
- No speeding.
- No skating against the direction of skating traffic.
- No roughhousing or shouting.
- Limit skating while holding hands to three skaters.

- Skates may be worn off the ice only in those rink areas covered with protective flooring. Avoid carpeted areas and bare concrete unless using skate guards.

Natural Ice and Ice Rescues

Skating outdoors on natural ice presents many hazards. Thin ice is the most dangerous condition. Rough ice or objects frozen in the ice, such as leaves, twigs, and stones, can cause tripping.

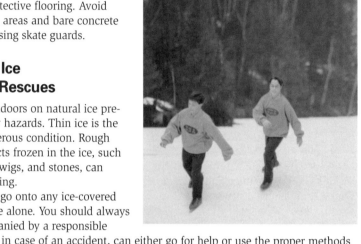

Never go onto any ice-covered water while alone. You should always be accompanied by a responsible adult who, in case of an accident, can either go for help or use the proper methods for rescuing persons who have fallen through the ice. As a Scout, you also should learn the methods of rescue for a person who has fallen through the ice.

Small bodies of water freeze more quickly than larger bodies, and the ice usually remains longer and generally provides a smoother, better skating surface. Ice formed over swift water or where water depth rises and falls is always unsafe. Ice must freeze to a uniform thickness of 4 inches before it is safe for skating or walking. Thawing ice is unsafe regardless of thickness.

There are at least two general rules that apply in all cases in which a person breaks through ice:

1. The person should not attempt to climb out immediately.

2. The victim should kick his feet to the surface to the rear to avoid jackknifing the body beneath the ice rim.

Rather than follow the first impulse to climb out after breaking through the ice, the person should extend the hands and arms forward on the unbroken surface, kick to nearly level position, and attempt to work forward onto the ice. If the ice breaks again, the victim should maintain his position and slide forward again. The victim, upon reaching firm ice, should not immediately stand, but should roll away from the break area, thus distributing the weight over as broad an area as possible on the weak ice.

Too often, when someone falls through ice, a would-be rescuer also breaks the ice in attempting to assist. Any equipment that helps distribute the weight of rescuers across a broader area of ice will help alleviate this problem. One of the most useful devices for ice rescue is a light ladder, from 14 to 18 feet long, with a light, strong line attached to the lowest rung. The ladder should be shoved out on the ice to the limit of its length with the line serving as an extension. If able to do so, the victim can climb onto the ladder and move along its length in a prone position.

If the victim is unable to climb onto the ladder, the rescuer may crawl out on the ladder to assist. If the ice breaks under the ladder, the ladder will angle upward from the broken ice area and can be drawn to safety by other persons.

For rescues in which the rescuer must remain at a distance from the victim because of ice conditions, a ring buoy with line attached or a coiled line with a weighted end may be thrown to the victim. A ring buoy can be skidded along the ice for a considerable distance.

A hockey stick with line attached can also be skidded along the ice. Sometimes a tree branch or board may be the only available device. A spare tire, preferably with line attached, may be used for an extension rescue and will support several people. In addition, a victim of ice accident may be rescued by use of a small flat-bottom boat shoved along the ice. The victim is pulled aboard over the stern.

Where no regular or improvised rescue devices are available, it may be necessary to form a human chain to effect a rescue. To form this chain, several rescuers approach as closely as they can with safety and then lie prone upon the ice, forming a "chain." Each person holds tightly to the skates or ankles of the person ahead of him. If possible, the lightest person should be closest to the victim. When the lead person grasps the victim, the person nearest shore pulls the others back. If the ice breaks under the weight of the lead person in the chain, the individual can be held and drawn to safety by the others.

Ask About Classes

Ask at an ice rink about ice skating classes for beginners. You will learn the right way from the start and avoid bad skating habits. Many rinks offer special Boy Scout skating classes at reduced prices.

Before your first visit to a rink, phone to inquire about session times and prices. Ask if some sessions are less crowded than others. If your Scout troop plans a visit, inquire about "group discount rates" and ask how many Scouts need to sign up in order to qualify for the group rate.

Both the Ice Skating Institute of America (the trade association of rink owners and operators) and the United States Figure Skating Association offer instructional programs and competition. USFSA activities are geared to the development of skaters at all levels, leading to world and Olympic competition.

Parts, Types, and Functions of Ice Skates

The Figure Skating Boot

Newcomers to ice skating seldom understand the importance of the figure skating boot; they frequently blame themselves for lack of skating ability when their problems come from wearing ill-fitting or poorly constructed boots.

Figure skating boots always should be made of leather. They should have

- A double sole

- An inner lining of leather (not cloth or plastic)

- A padded tongue

- An inner and outer strengthening stay running up the back of the boot

- Both eyelets and hooks

- A strong and durable counter—a type of stiffener built into the boot to support the ankle. (This is very important. Avoid using skating boots without counters.)

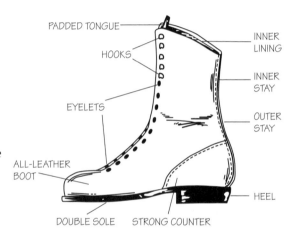

PADDED TONGUE

HOOKS

EYELETS

ALL-LEATHER BOOT

DOUBLE SOLE

STRONG COUNTER

INNER LINING

INNER STAY

OUTER STAY

HEEL

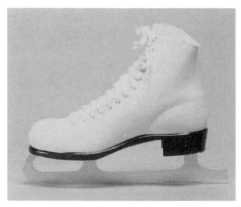

Figure Skates

Blade Design

There are three major factors in skating blade design:

- Speed
- Maneuverability
- Strength

It isn't possible to combine all three factors in one blade. The thinner the blade, the faster it will move, but a thin blade can't be as strong as a thicker one.

The more a blade is "rockered" (curved), the more maneuverable it will be, but it can't provide the same speed a flat, unrockered blade will give. This is because a rockered blade makes less blade contact with the ice as you thrust against it.

Figure skates need strong blades capable of withstanding the landings of high-speed jumps. The blades also must be exceptionally maneuverable. This is why figure blades are thick for strength and are heavily rockered. They can't provide great speed, but speed is not of greatest importance in figures, pairs skating, and freestyle.

Hockey skates need strong blades to withstand impact from pucks, hockey sticks, and other players' skates. They also need to provide speed, but they require only limited maneuverability. This is why hockey blades are thinner than figure skate blades, so they can offer more speed. At the same time, they can't be too thin or they could not withstand damage. They are rockered enough to provide limited maneuverability.

Speed blades don't need to be strong, since they will not be subject to impact from other sources, and they are seldom used for jumping (although barrel jumpers use speed skates). Speed skate blades can be made very thin to provide maximum speed. Speed blades have very little rocker—they don't need to be maneuverable, because speed skaters are not concerned with tight turns.

Blade designers have to compromise, depending on the type of blades they want. To gain more maneuverability and strength, they sacrifice a certain amount of speed. To gain more speed, they sacrifice a certain amount of strength and quite a bit of maneuverability.

Figure Blade Design

Figure skating blades are all similar in design, but there are several types for different purposes:

- General purpose recreational figure skates
- Special skates for compulsory figures
- Special skates for advanced jumps and spins (freestyle)
- Special skates for ice dancing

Four models of figure skating blades designed for these different kinds of figure skating are shown below.

General-Purpose Recreational Model

Compulsory Figures Model
The toe picks are smaller and higher than on the general-purpose model, and the blade has shallow precision hollow-ground edges.

Advanced Freestyle Model
The toe picks are larger, there is a special jumping pick, and the side-honed blade has deep hollow-ground edges.

Ice Dancing Model
The blade is thinner for high speed with minimum effort, and the shorter heel helps prevent tripping during intricate overlap footwork.

Hockey Blade Design

Types of hockey boots

Hockey players move forward and backward and turn at high speeds. Their blades are not designed to give the extreme maneuverability of figure skates. Hockey blades will have more "ice lay"—contact with the ice—than figure skates.

Since jumps, spins, and intricate footwork are never required, hockey blades have no toe picks and are smoothly curved at the toe. The blades are thinner than figure blades, since a thinner blade permits greater speed. Still they must be rugged enough to take hard impact.

The hockey boot has a hardened top cap, interior padding, and a high, extended back to prevent tendon damage. Although most hockey boots are made of leather, some manufacturers have introduced innovative, molded synthetic shell technology and offer removable inner linings. The hockey boot is similar, in many ways, to the modern ski boot.

We also are starting to see molded skate blade units made of thermoplastic nylon with the runners made of stainless steel.

The Speed Skate

Speed skate

These skates are designed for fast forward motion and possess little maneuverability. Since they are not subject to impact they can be made with thin blades, which permit greater speed. These blades have a projecting nose, beyond the front of the boot, to permit a longer "ice lay" (contact). They have almost no rocker, so are nearly flat against the ice. The boots are light in construction.

The clap skate was used in the 1998 Winter Olympics. Clap skate blades, which are connected only at the toe, allow the heels to lift off the skate. By keeping the blade on the ice longer and adding calf muscle to each stride, the clap skate trim's the speed skater's time. One major drawback exists: Skaters must adjust their technique for using the clap skate. That takes time.

Care of Boots and Blades

The leather used in figure, hockey, and speed skating boots must be kept clean and supple. Check the screws or rivets that attach the blades to the boots for tightness. Check the laces, and replace frayed laces promptly. Constantly check the blade edges for sharpness. After use, carefully dry boots and blades to prevent deterioration of leather and rusting of metal.

When carrying your skates, cover the blades with blade guards. When wearing skates off the ice, use the guards to protect the floor and your blades. Remove the guards before storing the skates to prevent blemishes from forming on the metal. Replace the rubber linings of boot tongues when they deteriorate.

Blades should be thoroughly dried with a towel at the end of each use. This will help prevent the blade from rusting. When storing skates between uses, place them in a bag so that the blades will not hit each other. (Terry cloth covers come in handy for storage of skates.)

When walking in the rink, use rubber guards to help protect the blades from knicks and scratches. Never wear skates while walking on cement.

When putting on or removing skates, loosen the laces so your foot will enter and leave the boot easily. Tugging the boot on or off can stretch the boot out of shape. Tuck the laces inside the boots after use.

Buying Ice Skates

Dry blades thoroughly.

Although rental skates are available at ice rinks, it's best to own your own well-fitted skates.

The most expensive set of boots and blades is not necessarily the best for you. The beginner doesn't need the expensive boots and specialized blades used by advanced skaters. When talking with a salesperson, be sure to describe accurately your present skating skills and how you will use your skates.

Expect new skates to feel stiff and somewhat uncomfortable. Don't buy skates that are too large for you. Well-fitted skates are essential.

Use terry cloth covers.

Ice Skating Skills

Starting on the Ice

When learning to ice skate, extend your arms forward and sideways so your hands are at waist height with palms downward. Keep your arms still, allowing a space between your upper arms and body. Stand upright, not leaning forward. Keep your knees slightly flexed—not stiff or overly flexed. Keep your feet about six inches apart and almost parallel, but with the toes turned slightly outward. With your feet still in this position, practice transferring your weight first onto one skate, then onto the other. Always keep your ankles close together, lifting one foot, then the other.

Push with left foot, forward glide on right foot, followed by two-footed parallel glide.

Alternating Pushes with Two-Footed Glides

After a minute or two of practicing weight transfers, stand with your heels together and toes turned outward in a V-position. Tilt the left skate inward slightly onto its inside edge, so it will grip the ice. Keep your back upright. Extend your arms at waist height, with your hands held palms downward. Slightly bend both knees and place your weight over the heel of the right foot.

Follow these steps.

- Apply sideways pressure on the left blade. This will cause the right skate to glide forward.

- Remove the left skate from the ice and bring the ankle of the left skate beside the ankle of the gliding right skate, allowing both skates to glide forward parallel to each other, with the blades vertical and upright.

Push with right foot, forward glide on left foot, followed by two-footed parallel glide.

- Now transfer your weight onto the heel section of the left skate and push sideways against the right skate's inside edge. This will cause the left skate to increase the forward motion.

- Remove the right skate from the ice and bring the ankle of the right skate close to the ankle of the gliding left skate, allowing both skates to glide forward parallel to each other.

- You'll maintain some forward momentum at this point. Keeping both feet on the ice and parallel to each other, glide on two feet until your forward motion is nearly ended.

Repeat what you have just done, but take four sideways pushes instead of only two. Always keep yourself balanced and in control.

Remember, after each sideways push, bring both feet together and parallel. Keep your arms from moving; moving your arms disturbs your balance.

When you can do four sideways pushes and two-footed glides without loss of stability or coordination, work on doing six in a row. Form is important. If you tend to push backward against the toe picks of the skates, don't increase the number of consecutive pushes yet. Practice properly. A few correctly executed pushes are worth twenty times the number of incorrect toe-pushes.

Always move gently. As you gain stability, keep increasing your number of consecutive pushes, from six to eight, then from eight to 10.

Learning to Stroke

Up to this point, you've made a sideways push and then immediately placed the pushing foot back onto the ice, to glide on two feet before starting the next push with the other foot. When you can do six or eight consecutive pushes without

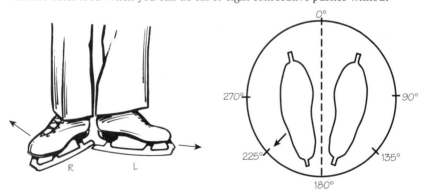

When stroking forward on ice skates, a sideways/backward push causes the inside edge of the pushing blade to cut down into the ice, forcing the blade of the other foot to move forward on a shallow outside edge. Never use the toe picks for pushing.

difficulty, try to shorten the length of time or the distance you glide on two feet after each push.

Eliminating these rests between strokes increases your speed and calls for well-timed transfers of weight as you step onto each gliding foot. Make your initial pushes gentle and try only four or five before taking a rest by going into a two-foot glide. When you can do six or eight strokes without losing coordination, you'll rapidly progress to double that number. Constantly check to make sure you never push backward against the toe picks, and your arms don't rise above waist height; keep your arms still. Also, bring your feet close together between each step. Do not develop a wide-legged stance.

Learn to anticipate your transfers of weight. As you transfer from one skate to the other, allow your weight to start moving over the next skate a little before it actually makes contact with the ice.

When you can accomplish 10 or 12 skating strokes without too much trouble, concentrate on making your movements smooth, with your back upright, your arms steady, your skating leg well flexed, and your free leg well extended. Develop good habits of style, posture, and rhythm.

Excess speed at this point will only harm your progress. Practice slower, steady, controlled skating during the early stages of learning. If you carefully perfect your basic skills, you'll soon be able to outdistance less patient beginners.

Forward skating does not create a pattern of straight lines on the ice. It actually creates a pattern of very shallow S-shaped curves. If you skate on perfectly clean ice, you should be able to see cuts on the ice which look like the illustration on the following page.

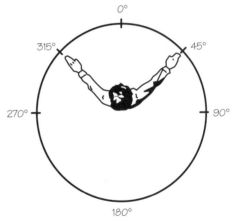

Above is an aerial view of the proper position of the arms in relation to the head when the skater is moving forward. The arms should never be held further back than 90/270 degrees. The hands should be held at waist height, with palms down, fingers together and extended.

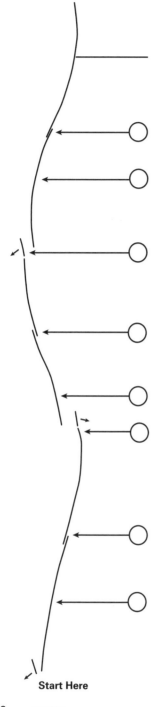

Step 1B repeats.

Step 1A repeats.

Step 3: The left foot, at the end of its glide, presses sideways to supply thrust.

Step 2B: The left foot edge changes from the outside edge to the inside edge as the skater begins to transfer weight toward the right leg, before actually stepping onto the right leg.

Step 2A: The left-foot glide begins on the shallow outside edge of the left blade.

Step 2: The right foot, at the end of its glide, presses sideways to supply thrust, making a deeper cut into the ice.

Step 1B: The right-foot edge changes to the inside edge as the skater begins to transfer weight toward the left leg, before actually stepping onto the left leg.

Step 1A: The right-foot glide begins on the shallow outside edge of the right blade.

Start Here

Step 1: The left blade presses downward and sideways against the ice to supply thrust.

Points to Remember

Always

- Keep your arms still.
- Keep your hands at waist height.
- Place your weight on the heel of the new skating foot as you step onto it (when skating forward).
- Push to the side, against the blade.
- Maintain a straight back.
- Bring the legs together between strokes.

Never

- Push backward, using the toe picks.
- Take a step without first placing your weight onto the skate.
- Allow the free foot to rise more than two or three inches above the ice.
- Skate with your hands in your pockets.
- Raise your arms if you begin to lose balance.
- Impede the flow of skate traffic; get up quickly if you fall.

The Two-Footed Snowplow Stop

Follow these steps.

- Glide forward on two feet. Keep your feet parallel and 12 inches apart. Your back should be straight, and your arms should be extended sideways and slightly forward, hands at waist height. Bend both knees while continuing to glide forward *in a straight line.*

- Push the heels of both skates outward at the same time, against very shallow inside edges of both blades. This causes both sets of toes to turn inward toward each other and both feet to incline inward slightly.

Two-Footed Snowplow Stop
Notice the extended arms, straight back, and bent knees. Start from a two-footed glide in a straight line forward. The blades' skidding action kicks in as the heels are forced outward on the inside edges and the toes turn inward.

- Apply pressure downward and sideways against both heels and both blades, causing the blades to start a skidding action on the ice. Keep your back upright (although as you first slow down, you'll tend to lean forward). Keep both knees bent throughout.

- Allow the skid to continue slowing until you eventually reach a complete stop without body movement. Do not move your arms from their extended position until three or four seconds after stopping. You should travel straight forward throughout the entire maneuver.

The One-Footed Snowplow Stop

Follow these steps.

- Glide forward on two feet. Keep your feet parallel and 12 inches apart. Your back should be straight. Extend your arms sideways and slightly forward, hands at waist height. Bend both knees while continuing to glide forward in a *straight line,* both blades vertical to the ice.

Starting a One-Footed Snowplow Stop
Begin the one-footed snowplow stop by gliding forward on two feet.

- While continuing the forward two-footed glide, transfer your weight onto your left foot. Although both skates continue to touch the ice, the greater part of your weight is now over your left foot.

- Keep the left blade quite vertical, so it continues to ride in a perfectly straight line. Allow both knees to increase their bend while you turn your right blade inward, onto its inside edge. (Remember, there should be almost no weight on the right blade.) The right toes should now be turned inward while the right heel is pushed outward.

- Gradually transfer weight from the left foot onto the right foot, making sure the left foot continues to ride in a straight line and the right

Finishing a One-Footed Snowplow Stop
Keep your back straight and extend your left arm in front of your stomach. Extend your right arm outward and backward. Keep your left knee well bent and keep the left blade upright while running it in a straight line.

Turn the right blade inward and skid against its inside edge.

foot continues to be turned toes-inward. As you transfer the weight, press downward and sideways against the right heel to make the blade of the right skate begin a skidding action on the ice.

- As you increase the skid with the right foot, let your left arm move forward until it is fully extended, with your left hand directly in front of your stomach. Let your right arm travel backward, fully extended, to end up pointing slightly backward.

- While skidding with the turned-inward right foot, be sure your left foot continues to be held upright, traveling over the ice in a straight line. Keep your back upright throughout the entire maneuver, but allow your left knee to bend freely as you continue the skidding action of the right blade.

- Continue the skid until you come to a complete stop. Do not allow your arms to move from their extended position until three or four seconds after you have stopped.

Gliding on Ice Skates

Forward Right-Foot Glide. Skate forward to gain a fair amount of speed. Interrupt your pushes and glide forward on both feet, keeping the blades upright, traveling in a straight line; your feet should be about 12 inches apart. Keep your arms still, your back upright, your knees slightly bent, and your shoulders level.

Without removing your left foot from the ice, transfer your weight to your right foot, making sure you continue to travel in a straight line.

Gently allow your left foot to travel forward in a straight line and lift it until it is no more than

Gliding

three inches off the ice. Keep your thighs close together and make sure the right blade remains upright, traveling straight. Carefully balance, allowing your right foot to continue onward, slightly increasing the bend of your right knee. See how far you can travel in a straight line.

Forward Left-Foot Glide. Start the maneuver again from the beginning. Gain speed, make a two-footed glide, gently transfer weight onto your left foot without taking your right foot from the ice. Once you transfer your weight, carefully move your right foot forward until it comes off the ice, allowing it to rise no more than three inches above the ice surface. Make sure you skate in a straight line throughout the entire maneuver. Keep your back straight and arms extended.

Stroking

Requirement 2b for ice skating asks you to start from a T position and stroke forward. In the T position, your front foot points straight forward. Your back foot is turned outward with the instep against the heel of the front foot. Now you're prepared to push off with the back foot and glide forward on the front skate.

Your counselor will be looking for good style and coordination rather than speed. You should try to avoid toe-pushing and double-tracking between strokes (resting on two feet between alternating pushes is called double-tracking). The skating leg should bend each time you step onto a foot, and the free leg should extend every time you remove it from the ice. Don't look down at the ice. Keep your back upright, and keep your arms controlled, extended, and waist high.

When skating around corners, lean into the curve, extending your outside arm forward so your hand is in front of your stomach. The inside arm and shoulder should be pulled horizontally backward. During the merit badge review, you may skate around curves on two feet, or by stroking, or by performing forward crossovers.

T position

Stroking

Gliding Backward

You may choose your own method of gaining speed in a backward direction before starting your glide on two feet.

With the **scissors method**, you keep both blades on the ice. With your skate toes together and heels angled out 45 degrees apart, use side pressure on the inside of each skate to force your feet apart to a distance roughly equal to your shoulder width. At this point, with continued pressure on the inside of the skates, your heels should turn inward until they are about three inches apart. Then the blades run parallel. Repeat this movement, heels going out and then pulling back in, with a continuous, unhurried, rhythmic action.

Two-footed glide

When you skate backward, you place your weight over the ball of each foot.

(In forward skating it's over the heel of the foot.) Keep your back straight, bending your knees slightly. Keep your arms extended slightly forward with plenty of space between your upper arms and body. Hold your hands at waist height, palms down. Your wrists should not droop. Don't twist your head to see where you're going. That will cause your body to turn, and you may lose your balance. Arrange for a friend to skate in front of you, to warn you if you're skating too close to other skaters or the rink fence. Resist the tendency to bend forward to look at your skates.

Some skating instructors don't like the scissors method because it leaves both skates on the ice and places the skater on the inside edges of the blades. In the more accepted method of backward skating, the skater lifts each skate off the ice separately, just as in forward skating. Each backward step begins on an outside edge rather than an inside edge.

The scissors method, however, provides a simple way for a beginner to become familiar with the sensation of backward movement. It provides more stability and lets you build up enough speed to do a backward glide on both feet.

Once you gain speed, bring both skates to a parallel position about 12 inches apart, with the blades running upright and the weight on the ball of each foot. Bend your knees slightly, keep your arms still and extended and your back upright. The blades should run in a straight line backward. The requirement asks you to glide for at least 25 feet, so practice building up enough speed to sustain the glide.

Skating Backward

Skating Backward

To complete this requirement, you must skate backward for a distance to be determined by your counselor (not less than 40 feet nor more than 100 feet). If you use the scissors method for skating backward, try to progress to the higher level of skill in which you lift each skate off the ice separately. To do this, you must transfer the weight onto each foot in turn as it contacts the ice.

First experiment with transferring your weight. Stand with your toes touching and your heels about eight inches apart. Without moving from where you are, lift one foot from the ice and put it down. Then lift the other foot and put it down. Make sure your toes remain close together and heels apart, so you are pigeon-toed. Whenever you place a foot on the ice, let the outside edge of your blade touch the ice by slightly angling your foot outward. Don't look down, keep your back upright, and keep your arms extended and still.

Even though you may not be attempting to move backward while you experiment with these transfers of weight, a backward movement will probably start by itself. Allow the movement to progress, but before placing a skate on the ice, make sure you place the toes of your skates close together to avoid any tendency for your legs to move wider apart. Stay pigeon-toed. Make four separate steps backward and then allow both blades to run on the ice to stabilize your balance and slow you down.

Go back to the pigeon-toe position. Keep your toes together and your back upright. Transfer weight from foot to foot as you step onto the ice for six steps before resting on two feet. Develop the number of steps you can take. Once you can take 10 successive steps, you'll progress rapidly to double that number. You'll be well on your way to becoming a proficient backward skater.

Each time you step, remember to place the toes of your skates together. Otherwise, your legs will get farther apart and you won't be able to step onto a shallow outside edge each time.

Glide and Turn

Skating forward on two feet in a curving arc is sometimes called a hockey glide, since hockey players use this maneuver.

Follow these steps for the **left hockey glide.**

- Gain adequate speed and then interrupt your skating strokes to rest on two feet in a straightforward two-footed glide.

- To curve to the left, slide the left foot forward, keeping it parallel to the right foot and one boot length ahead of the right boot. Roll the left foot outward so a firm cut is made into the ice with the outside edge of the blade of the left skate.

- At the same time, lean to the left, rotating your upper body with a firm, strong movement. Allow both arms to rotate to the left, so your left arm is fully extended behind you and your right arm is fully extended in front of your stomach.

- Keep your feet parallel, the left foot in front of the right. Don't twist the left (leading) foot to the left. This will cause the left foot to jar and possibly to skid.

- Don't lean out of the curve—lean inward. And remember, the whole upper body must rotate, not just the arms.

- To come out of the curve and resume movement in a straight line, straighten up from your lean, let your arms return to their normal position, extended to the sides of the body. Straighten your blades so they are vertical to the ice.

Follow these steps for the **right hockey glide.** After performing your hockey glide to the left for 180 degrees around a cone placed on the ice, you'll perform it to the right.

- First gain speed skating forward, then interrupt your stroking to go into a straight two-footed glide.

- Push your right foot forward one booth length in front of the left boot, keeping both feet parallel.

- Just before you reach the cone, drop the right boot over so the outside edge of the right blade cuts firmly into the ice. Lean to the right, and allow the upper body and both arms to rotate strongly to the right.

- Maintain that position throughout the 180-degree curve around the cone and then straighten up. Let both blades run in a vertical position.

- Bring your arms and body to the normal forward-skating positions as you resume movement in a straight line.

Shoot-the-Duck

This maneuver greatly strengthens the stomach and thigh muscles and improves balance.

- First you gain speed, then go into a two-footed glide in a straight line. Make sure you are running on the flat (all four edges), so you won't start curving.

- Advance one leg forward of the other, transferring your weight to the foot in the rear.

Shoot-the-Duck

- Once you transfer your weight, let the front foot rise from the ice, keeping it only 3 or 4 inches above the ice surface while bending the rear knee as fully as possible.

- Keep both arms fully extended, and move forward so your hands are in front of your stomach. Keep your back as straight as possible and your shoulders level to keep from toppling sideways.

- Continue bending your rear knee until your buttocks are close to (but not touching) the skate running on the ice.

    Getting up from a shoot-the-duck position requires strong muscles in the thighs and the stomach.

- Rise up on your skating leg, letting both arms push forward slightly. This keeps your arms from rising and causing a backward fall.

- Don't allow the free foot to rise more than six inches above the ice throughout the entire maneuver.

- Once you're up, return your arms to the usual forward-skating position and glide forward on both feet.

When first learning shoot-the-duck, you may prefer to bend down while on two feet, then lift one foot from the ice and replace it before getting up. This method places less strain on your muscles. If you do this, push your arms forward both when removing the foot from the ice and when replacing it, to prevent a backward fall.

You may use either method in merit badge tests. Practice shoot-the-duck at home, without skates, to strengthen muscles.

Crossovers: The Figure 8

The crossover teaches you how to skate a curving path, for example, around the end of an ice rink.

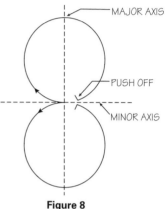

Figure 8

You should learn forward crossovers in circles about 25 feet in diameter. Crossovers involve skating around the circle, making normal strokes onto the outside edge of the skate that is on the inside of the circle, then crossing the outer skate around the front of the inner skate and placing the outer skate on the ice on its inside edge. The term "crossover" is not really accurate, because the foot does not cross over the inner foot; it crosses in front of it.

To make a forward crossover in a counterclockwise circle:

- Rotate the upper part of your body toward the inside of the circle. At the same time, rotate both arms firmly to the left, so your left arm is extended behind you and your right arm is extended in front of your stomach. Your palms should face downward, and your wrists should not droop.

- Pushing sideways against the right blade, step with your left foot, leaning into the circle so the left blade is on its outside edge as it rides over the ice. Keep your arms and hands in their correct positions. Don't let them move.

- As your right foot leaves the ice, take it around the front of your left skate, keeping the blade not more than an inch or two above ice level. Take it so far around the left foot that the calf of the right touches the shin of the left leg. When it is fully around, step down onto the right inside edge.

- As you step onto the right skate, lift the left foot from the ice, toes first. Keep the heel no more than an inch or so from the ice. This prevents the left toe picks from digging into the ice and greatly enhances the appearance of the maneuver.

- Don't let the left blade rise more than an inch or two above the ice level. Bring your left foot around the rear of your right foot until your left foot is parallel and very close to your right foot. Then step onto your left foot, pushing sideways against the right blade to supply thrust.

Repeat the sequence of movements. If you lose coordination, run on a curving two-footed glide for a while to restore balance, and then try again. At first, you may find it difficult to perform more than two or three consecutive crossovers. After a little practice you'll be able to make several crossovers, but you may be toe-pushing. Resist toe-pushes when doing crossovers, as the habit is hard to break.

When you can successfully perform crossovers in a counterclockwise direction, learn to do them in a clockwise direction. When skating around a circle to the right, lean to the right, rotate the body and arms fully to the right, and allow the left foot to make the crossing process.

**Forward Crossover
(Right foot around left)**

When you can crossover in each direction, practice in a figure-eight pattern, first completing a full circle counterclockwise and then changing direction into a full circle clockwise. When making the change of direction, you may simply glide on two feet forward before changing your lean and your body and arm positions as you start skating into the new circle.

Forward crossovers are among the most important basic skating skills. It's important to perform them equally well in each direction. Most skaters find it easier to learn them counterclockwise, since in most rinks the public skating sessions are run in a counterclockwise direction.

Racing on Ice

Racing is always fun, but safety comes first. It's best to run the race on an oval track rather than racing down the center of a rink, where you may be faced with a solid wooden wall just when you're at maximum speed. On an oval course, the finish line should be about one third of the distance along one of the long sides of the oval. Plenty of ice space is then available for slowing down after you cross the line.

Racing skaters should wear gloves to protect their hands and fingers from other skaters' blades in the event of spills. Rules should be established, such as "no pushing, no tripping," etc. Skaters should be warned that if they fall, they should immediately get onto their feet again, taking care to avoid unnecessary ice contact with hands.

Requirement 2d for ice skating asks you to take part in a relay race. Your counselor will explain the set-up and the rules.

Hockey Stop

Hockey Stop

The hockey stop is one of the best ways to stop quickly when you're skating forward.

For requirement 2d for ice skating, you'll make a complete stop using both feet in a skidding action. The hockey stop must be performed in a straight line. Practice slowly at first.

- Stroke forward to build up some speed, then glide on two feet.

- Bring your feet close together, bend your knees, and turn your feet crosswise (90 degrees) to your direction of travel. Meanwhile, your shoulders should face the line of travel. (See the photo above.)

- At the same time, lean back slightly. This puts your front skate on its inside edge and your back skate on its outside edge. The result is a skidding action that brings you to a stop.

- Keep your feet parallel. Your head, shoulders, and torso should be parallel to your feet at the conclusion of the hockey stop.

- Bend your knees more deeply to produce a faster stop.

ROLLER SKATING

Tips for the Beginner

It's important to learn the fundamentals of roller skating correctly at the beginning, so you can avoid bad habits that are hard to break. Ask about skating classes at your rink. You'll benefit greatly from attention by a skilled skating instructor.

Don't Walk—Skate

Habit is difficult to overcome, so don't start "walking" on your skates. A walking movement sends your leading foot out in front of your body, pitching your body weight forward. This results in your supporting skate sliding out behind you.

To learn the correct method, try to visualize one skate as the carrier of the body. You propel yourself forward with a slight push from your other leg.

Proper follow-through ensures smooth, steady skating.

Follow-Through

Baseball players, golfers, and other athletes devote much time and attention to improvement of their follow-through. Follow-through is important to skaters, too.

The most efficient pushing stroke on roller skates begins with your body upright, knees slightly bent, and skates underneath the body and parallel.

- Put your weight on the pushing skate and begin the push out to the side and back, using pressure on the inside of the pushing skate. This propels the carrying skate forward. Use the entire leg in the pushing movement, not merely the lower leg.

- Keep the pushing skate on the floor with enough body weight on it to ensure the longest possible push. The pushing skate should be in contact with the skating surface as long as possible. See page 44, left and center photos.

- Gradually transfer your body weight to the carrying skate as you leave the pushing skate behind. You'll glide forward with your weight on the carrying leg, which is called the **skating leg**.

- Keep your pushing foot on the surface until your knee straightens and the foot flows off the floor into a carried position. Once your pushing leg is clear of the skating surface, it becomes the **free leg** or balance leg. (Don't use a kicking motion as you lift it from the skating surface, since this deprives you of a full push.)

- When your free leg becomes the carrier, the knee bends and the skate glides forward alongside the other skate. Repeat the process. See photos on page 44.

Forward Scissors Movement

With the scissors movement, a new skater can keep both skates in contact with the skating surface while learning to skate forward.

- Balance evenly over the centers of both skates. Maintain a firm upright body carriage.

- Keeping your back straight, bend both knees slightly by dropping them forward toward the toes. (But avoid a sitting position.)

- With your heels together and toes angled about 45 degrees apart, use sideways pressure on the inside of each skate to force the feet to a shoulder distance apart.

- At this point, pull the skates in again, with pressure to the inside of the skates and toes turned inward (pigeon-toed).

- The skates should pull back together until they are roughly two inches apart. Repeat this movement (out and in), with continuous, unhurried action.

The scissors movement trains you to support your body while in motion, and you gain valuable experience in using side push movement. See the photos below.

Forward Scissors

Aiming the Skates

The curved skating path that results from proper body lean is called an edge. This is the way all good skaters travel around the rink, in a counterclockwise direction.

When a skater leans away from his free leg, his skating foot is on an **outside edge**. A body lean toward the free-leg side puts the skater on an **inside edge**.

As you round the ends of the rink, leaning in the direction of the floor's center, your skates follow a constant arc. This is the result of left outside forward edges and right inside forward edges.

Safety

Rules and Etiquette

Shake each skate. Are there any rattles? Does anything feel loose? If so, investigate and have the trouble corrected. A loose wheel or skate assembly can separate from your skate, causing a spill.

Check to see if your boots are properly laced and securely tied. A loose bootlace can foul your wheels and cause an accident.

A thoughtful and courteous skater will find the roller rink an easy place to make friends. Learn the house rules. Fast skating, weaving suddenly in and out of the normal flow of skating, uncontrolled skating movements, and trick skating are usually forbidden because they endanger other skaters.

The average speed of the majority of skaters at a rink should be your maximum speed. Any skater who consistently passes more skaters than pass him is skating too fast.

Be respectful of other skaters and use care in passing. Be especially careful of beginners and young children.

Be sure you review and learn the BSA skating guidelines that appear in "Note to Counselor" at the beginning of this book.

Rink Rules

Each roller rink has rules posted, so read them before skating. Some typical rules:

- No speed skating during public skating sessions.
- No tag or follow-the-leader.
- No crack-the-whip.
- No roughhousing of any kind.
- No eating or drinking while on the skating surface.

Equipment and Care of Skates

Skate Parts and Functions of Skates

The rubber cushion assembly on the bottom of a roller skate allows the skate to be steered through side pressure on the wheels. This lets you skate forward, skate backward, and turn.

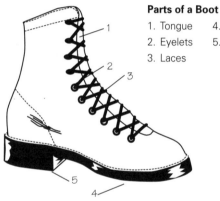

Parts of a Boot

1. Tongue   4. Sole
2. Eyelets   5. Heel
3. Laces

Parts of a Roller Skate

1. Toe stop	4. Axle	7. Hanger
2. Truck	5. Cushions	8. Plate
3. King pin	6. Wheels	9. Jump bar
	(a) Loose ball bearing	10. Hex nut
	(b) Precision bearing	11. Pivot pin
		12. Retainer cap
		13. Allen screw
		14. Dust cap
		15. Axle nut
		16. Rivet

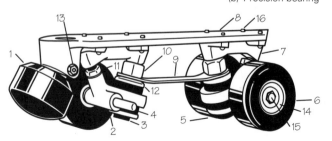

Equipment

Rental shoe skates are available at the rink, though it's best to own your skates if you plan to take lessons and are reasonably sure that you intend to keep skating long enough to justify the expense. A well-fitted skate is a must in order to become a good skater. Buy the best skate you can afford, and buy from people who are experienced in the business of roller skating. They are qualified to fit you with the proper size, and they can explain the differences in the quality of boots, plates, toe stops, and wheels. They usually have a guarantee on their skates, and they may have a trade-in allowance if you outgrow them. They also can adjust the skates and provide replacement parts.

If your budget is very limited, check local shops and rinks, which may post notices about used skates for sale. Your parent can help you make wise decisions when purchasing skates and other equipment.

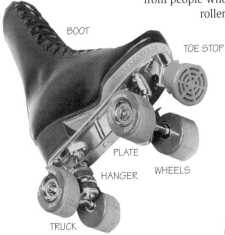

BOOT
TOE STOP
PLATE
HANGER   WHEELS
TRUCK

Care of Skates

1. No skate should ever be used before it is oiled or lubricated. Ball-bearing skates are oiled. A drop of oil in the bearings, on each side of each wheel, should last for 10 wearings. Precision skates are lubricated with a special lubricant, and this work should be done by a rink mechanic every six months.

2. Use a leather softener and preserver on your boots every six months. Polish the boots regularly to preserve them and enhance their appearance.

3. When removing your skates, unlace them until they slip off easily. Put laces inside. Tugging on your boot when you put it on or remove it will stretch your boot out of shape.

4. Before you skate, make sure all nuts are on tight, especially the wheel nuts.

5. Do not let toe stops wear down to the point where the metal parts or nails cut up the floor.

How to Start

Forward Skating
Foot moves to the rear of body

How to Stop

Roller Skating Skills

Skating Forward: How to Start

Most skating strokes start from the same position—the **T position.** You start with your feet close together, with the right skate placed behind the left heel, as shown at **left.**

You transfer your weight to your left skate as you push with your right skate, which moves to the rear. At the end of a comfortable distance of travel, give a push with the big toe, which is usually enough to maintain momentum until you can take the next stroke. The pushing right foot returns to the parallel position, and the left foot then moves to the rear with the next push. (For more about pushing technique, review the earlier sections, "Don't Walk—Skate" and "Follow-Through.")

Practice forward skating in both directions around the rink. Also practice skating forward and gliding on one skate, then on the other skate.

How to Stop

Stopping on skates is a fairly simple procedure but one that requires caution at first.

The T-stop uses the wheels as a source of friction.

- Stand still with the right skate placed behind the heel of the left one in a T position.

- Keeping the body upright, bend both knees slightly and push off easily onto the left skate. Maintain firm support of your upper body.

- Return the right skate to the T position but off the floor, pressing the middle of the skate into the heel of the left.

- *Gradually* lower the right skate onto the skating surface, keeping the skates pressed together, and *slowly* transfer your body weight to the right skate. The friction of the right skate on the skating surface is the braking factor, since the wheels are not in a position to roll.

There are several variations of this stopping method, all of them using side friction.

You'll notice a tendency to lunge forward while stopping. Try to resist this by supporting your body with a firm back and leaning very slightly away from your direction of travel until your skates come to a halt. The stopping action should be gradual and controlled, not quick. If you try to stop suddenly, the top part of your body will pitch forward.

Skating Backward

Most new roller skaters view the ability to skate backward as the ultimate skating experience. When you can skate forward with ease, you'll have no trouble learning to skate backward. The balance and poise you learned during forward skating is completely transferable to backward skating. All the principles of skate movement are the same, with only a few changes.

Use the buddy system when you start backward skating. Have a friend stand in front of you and skate forward, supporting you by placing his hands under your elbows. Rest your forearms on top of his. Then, after you master skating backward on two feet, practice skating backward on one foot.

The buddy system

Use the Scissors

Scissors is once again the best way to start in this new direction. Stand erect, without bending forward at the waist, and balance your weight evenly over the center of both skates. Resist the common tendency to look down and watch your skate movements.

The main difference in forward and backward scissors is that the toe-in positions are reversed.

- Begin the movement with toes inward (pigeon-toed).

- Drive the skates apart about shoulder width and then bring them together with the heels leading inward.

- Maintain pressure to the inside of both skates. Action should be unhurried but continuous.

One-foot Stroking

Once you master the backward scissors movement, it's a simple matter to convert to one-foot stroking, using a side pressure push to the front of the body.

- While gliding backward, bring your feet together and parallel.

- Shift the weight to one foot and let the other foot travel to the front of the body.

- After a short distance, give a push with the big toe of the front foot to continue motion, then return your foot to the parallel position.

Repeat the backward stroke with the other foot. The illustration here shows this pattern on the floor.

Backward Skating
Foot moves to front of body

Crosscutting on Skates

The picture below shows two Scouts doing the left cross in front stroke. The illustration below shows a right-cross pattern on the floor.

With your feet parallel, lift the right foot and place it on the floor to the left of the left foot and slightly in front. Move the left foot to the rear and raise it from the floor. Continue cross in fronts by placing the left foot to the right of the right foot.

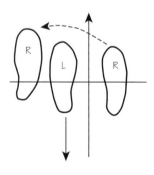

Right cross in front

Left cross in front

Skating a Slalom Pattern

The illustration at right shows skating the slalom pattern. This is a serpentine movement, following a course laid out on the skating surface. Try it first by skating on both feet, with skates parallel. After you master skating slalom style on two feet, practice lifting one foot and keeping within the markers on the floor.

Start

Skating the Slalom Backward

While skating backward on two feet, skate a slalom pattern as shown at left. Advanced skaters can try this on one foot, then on the other foot.

Start

Shuttle Skating

In this test you skate at varying speeds around the rink and maintain balance while bending over to pick up an object from the rink floor.

Four blocks or similar objects are placed on the rink surface, one at each corner. Four containers are spaced at equal distances away from the blocks. You must skate around the rink and pick up each object and deposit it in the next container. See the illustration below.

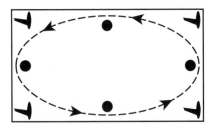

The Wide Spread Eagle

The wide spread eagle is a basic position in skating that leads to doing two-footed turns properly. The position is shown in the picture to the left; the right skate traveling forward, the left backward. After accomplishing this position, the skater gradually brings his feet closer together until the heels are touching, if he can. This is the basic position for several fundamental turns in skating.

Mohawk

You can use this turn to change from forward skating to backward skating. You'll still be traveling in the same direction when you complete the turn. The Mohawk uses a variation of the wide spread eagle.

1. The skater in the photo at left begins by skating forward on his left foot.

2. He turns his shoulders and hips in the direction he wants to turn. He places his free (right) foot on the floor in the direction of backward skating.

3. He picks up his left foot and either holds it to the rear or places it alongside the right foot, which is now gliding backward. He's ready to take the next stroke.

Turning from backward skating to frontward skating uses the same technique, but reversed.

Spinning on Skates

A wide variety of spins are possible on roller skates. One of the easiest to learn is the heel-and-toe spin. Begin by standing erect with your skates under your body, aligned approximately three to four inches apart. Extend your arms to the side, straight out from the shoulders. Take a deep breath to raise your rib cage. Straighten your back, look forward (not down), and hold the body firmly erect without stiffness.

The remaining instructions assume you are right-handed. If you're left-handed, change *left* and *right* in the instructions.

- Without raising any wheels from the skating surface, apply pressure to the front set of wheels on the left skate and rear wheels on the right.

- While not allowing the lower body or skates to move, slowly rotate your upper body, shoulders, and arms clockwise (right) to a "cocked" position, preliminary to triggering your spin.

- With upper body unity, start the spin by snapping your arms and torso into a counterclockwise direction (right to left), permitting the lower body and skates to follow. Keep pressure on the right-heel and left-toe wheels of your skates.

Balance is of critical importance to spinning. Retain your erect body position throughout. Your first attempts should be taken slowly and carefully, with only one or two turns until you develop greater skill through practice. Drawing your arms slowly inward toward your body will increase spinning speed.

Hop, Skip, and Jump on Skates

This is a three-part requirement. The first part of the hop consists of just that, hopping on one foot a short distance above the floor.

The second part is also known as a bunny hop. It consists of "digging" one skate, or pushing the skate toe stop sharply into the floor, and hopping to the other skate.

These moves can be demonstrated much better by your counselor but are illustrated here by the two pictures below.

The third part of this requirement is the jump. It is often called a waltz jump. The three pictures on page 58 illustrate the three phases of this jump. The jump consists of taking off from one foot, turning the body while in the air, and landing on the other foot in the opposite direction from which the takeoff was made.

Hop

Skip

Jump

Takeoff

In the air

Landing

Racing on a Speed Track

Speed skating or racing is a popular part of roller skating, but one that must be practiced and skated under highly controlled conditions. As in all sports where speed is the object, high speed limits a person's ability to change directions or stop to avoid a collision with an obstacle or another participant. For these reasons, good Scouts must never go fast when other skaters are in the rink at the same time. Speed skating and racing are generally done in rinks at times set aside for that purpose only.

Using the skills you have learned so far will help you refine and practice the techniques and rules of speed skating. With help from your counselor, you will be able to demonstrate correct technique in starting, cornering, passing, and pacing.

The first picture above shows two Scouts on the starting line ready to take off in a race, and the second one shows them rounding a pylon or corner in the proper manner.

Shoot-the-Duck

The pictures below illustrate the steps in learning the shoot-the-duck.

- First use fast stroking to build up speed.

- Bend over and touch your toes.

- Bend down in a squatting position, with your hands extended directly forward.

- Extend one leg out in front, assisting by placing your hands under the knee of your extended leg.

- When you're nearly stopped, rise into an upright position by reversing the procedure. After some practice, you should be able to rise while on one foot.

You can learn to skate slalom pattern while in the shoot-the-duck position. You can also shoot-the-duck while skating backward, but you must take extreme care to avoid collisions.

Limbo Under

The picture illustrates the entire procedure. While skating forward, the skater leans back and skates under a bar: the lower the bar, the more skilled the limbo skater. If you can go under the bar in the shoot-the-duck position, this will help you pass under a lower bar.

The Stepover

The picture below is a good illustration of requirement 2e for roller skating. The Scout skates slowly and steps over the bar.

Dribbling a Basketball

For this requirement, you should be able to dribble the ball the length of the floor, turn around, and come back to your starting point. This also can be done in teams.

Hockey Puck on Skates

Practice skating completely around the rink, using a hockey stick to push the puck in front of you. Pushing too hard will lessen your control. Skating at an even speed and pushing the puck smoothly will help keep the puck in control.

IN-LINE SKATING

Tips for the Beginner

Along with the excitement of learning how to skate, many new skaters fear injury. However, you can learn to skate without injuring yourself. First pay close attention to grasping the basics. That will help your confidence as you learn each skating skill. Before you know it, you'll be skating like an expert!

If you've never been on skates before, it's a good idea to start out on a soft, level surface. Dry grass or even the carpet inside your home are both good choices.

Getting Comfortable on your Skates

First, sit on a sturdy surface and put on your safety gear and skates. (*Always* wear your safety gear, no matter where you're skating.) Sitting at the edge of your seat, position your skates with toes out, heels touching. This is called the **V-stance**.

Holding onto the chair, rise in one smooth motion and center your hips over your heels. While you do the next exercise, keep your head up and facing forward. Get used to the feel of the skates underneath you without looking down at them.

V-stance

Positions (Stances)

Place your feet apart, shoulder-width, and raise your hands to waist level. Slightly bend your hips, knees, and ankles. You'll go down a few inches when you do this. Imagine a line connecting your shoulders, hips, and ankles. Keep your weight distributed this way, and you'll be much less apt to fall. This position is called the **ready position**.

In the ready position, test the way your body moves. Lean forward and backward, remembering to keep your knees bent. Try sinking several inches and rising up again a few times. Notice how the pressure changes with your body's movements?

Ready position (front)

Ready position (side)

Bend your knees carefully until you can touch them—then go ahead and touch your toes! See how easy it is to move around in your skates? Tip the skate wheels to the right and then to the left to gain confidence in the support in-line skates offer.

Tip: Keep your knees bent and your pelvis tucked forward whenever you're on in-line skates. In this position you're ready to react in different situations.

Now stand with your skates a little more than shoulder distance apart. This is known as the **A-frame stance**. Practice tipping your skates inward, then

A-Frame Stance

return to the normal A-frame stance. Do the same thing except tip the skates outward. In the A-frame stance, put your toes as close together as possible without hurting and heels out. This is known as the **A-stance**.

To stand still, use the **Safe-T**. Roll the skate without the brake back until it touches the arch of the other skate, making a T-shape. Practice this until you feel securely anchored in the Safe-T.

Safe-T

Falling Down

With good skating skills and the proper safety attitude and equipment, falling shouldn't be a problem. However, if you feel a fall coming, try to fall forward—so your wrist guards, elbow guards, and knee pads will provide some protection.

Getting up

Getting Up

If you do end up on the ground, you need a way back up, don't you? No problem. To get up:

1. Get on hands and knees.

2. Raise one knee and put that skate on the ground close to your other knee.

3. Keeping your upper body upright, sit on the heel of the other skate. Center yourself directly over both skates, so your skates won't roll out from under you.

4. Use your hands on the raised knee to push yourself straight up in one smooth motion.

V-Walk, or Duck Walk

This exercise helps you get a feel for your inside wheel edges. it's also the next step you take toward skating:

1. Put your toes out, heels touching.

2. Lift one skate at a time, stepping in place and shifting your weight right, then left, and so on.

3. Now advance each skate a few inches ahead as you step and shift your weight. With your feet still in the V-stance, you'll waddle like a duck.

Crab Walk

This step helps you gain confidence on your skates. You'll also use it later to perform crossovers. The effect you're trying to achieve here is walking your skates to the left while facing forward. You'll also repeat the walk to the right.

1. Stand in the ready position. If possible, find a line to stand on. Stand on the line so it's passing from your left to right (not between the skates).

2. With your arms raised in the ready position, look toward the left and rotate your shoulders in that direction.

3. Pass the right skate over the left skate and place it back on the line, on the other side of the left skate. Let your left ankle completely relax onto its left side to give your right foot plenty of room.

4. Bring the left skate from behind the right and place it in its natural place (to the left of the right foot) on the line.

5. Keep walking down the line to the left until you're comfortable with the crab walk.

6. Practice the same steps to the right until you're back at your original position.

The Glide

Now try skating on dry grass (or carpet).

1. Put your feet in the Safe-T position.

2. Tip the back skate onto the inside edge and push against that edge.

3. Lean your upper body over the knee of the front skate and lunge forward over that knee.

4. When your weight transfers to the front skate, pick up the back skate and move it forward, closing the gap between the skates.

Practice by repeating again and again.

Skating Know-How

Good in-line skating skills are as important a part of skating safety as good equipment. Now that you have the required gear, learn good skills. Think about this: all the safety equipment in the world won't help you if you head down a steep hill without knowing how to stop when you get to the bottom!

Until you have full command of the basics, avoid busy areas where you may find more experienced skaters. Stay in a controlled, flat environment where you can learn without outside pressure. First learn the basics very, very well: speed control, turning, braking, and stopping.

Smart Skating

You'll learn good skating skills, but you also need to have a smart skating attitude. One requirement for the Skating merit badge is to state skating safety rules, and you must also know how to safely pass a pedestrian. All safety rules fall under skating etiquette, which is really common sense:

- *Most of all, always control yourself. Always be in control of your skates and have a good, safe skating attitude. Don't be a show-off.*

- Stay on the right side of the path. Always pass on the left, and always call out a warning, "Passing on left!"

- Skate with the flow of traffic.

- Don't wear headphones!

- Legally, you are a wheeled vehicle. Learn and observe all traffic regulations. Remember to yield to pedestrians.

- Stay away from anything on the road surface, including water, oil, and rocks. These make an unsafe skating surface and can damage your skates or cause them to wear early.

- Avoid heavy traffic.

- Take care where you skate alone. Don't ever leave yourself open to danger by skating in run-down areas after dark.

- If you do skate after dark, make sure your equipment and skates are well-covered with reflective material that shows up in the dark. In fact, it's a good idea to apply reflective material when you first begin to skate. You never know when you might stay out later than you plan.

- Skate only where you know you are welcome. If you're skating in a park, make sure the park allows in-line skating and you're skating in an area that isn't off-limits to in-line skaters. Don't ever skate on private property unless you have the owner's permission. Never wear your skates inside a business or some-one else's home.

When you skate in groups:

- Don't give in to peer pressure to skate beyond your level.

- Look out for one another.

- Give each other plenty of room to move.

- Let an experienced skater bring up the rear.

Safety

Many people would never consider learning to in-line skate because they fear injury. What they don't realize is that most safety concerns are within your control. Take safety seriously. You control your own safety by

- Always using protective gear and properly functioning skates
- Knowing and practicing good in-line skating skills
- Having a safe, smart attitude

Be sure you review and learn the BSA skating guidelines that appear in "Note to Counselor" at the beginning of this book.

Gearing Up for Safety

Protective Gear

To minimize injury and make skating a pleasurable, fun pastime, in-line skating uses a great deal of protective gear. Properly equip yourself for safe in-line skating by wearing a helmet, wrist guards, elbow guards, and knee pads.

Always wear your helmet. Besides wearing it for protection, wear it to set a good example, to increase your confidence, and to make you more obvious to motorists. And one of the most important reasons to wear it is that it's required by law in many cities and states.

Wrist guards are also extremely important. Far and away, the most common skating injury treated is injury to the wrist, followed by injuries to the lower arm. Your natural reaction when you feel a fall coming is to put your hands out to catch yourself. Wrist guards help reduce the risk of injury.

You should also use elbow guards and knee pads. You'll be more willing to try a new turn when you know you'll be protected if you take a

Smart in-line skaters take safety seriously and always wear protective gear.

spill. Purchase the best safety equipment you can afford, knowing that the better and more complete your equipment is, the more confident a skater you will become. Also, well-made equipment lasts longer, and its parts are more practical to replace—making it the best bargain in the long run.

When you're shopping for equipment, hold a pair of inexpensively made wrist guards in one hand and a pair of higher-quality wrist guards in the other. Consider the different materials. Is the plastic protective area rigid and hard—will it protect you if you fall? Or is it so thin and flimsy you can bend it with very little pressure? Are the connective materials—straps and so on—secure and sturdy? Are the fabric fastener strips wide, and are they sewn with heavy, fine stitching? You want safety equipment that can stand up to the impact of a fall. Poor equipment is probably worse than no equipment, because it may give you a false sense of security.

Choosing Skates for Safety and a Smooth Ride

For safety's sake, the skate itself obviously should be the best you can afford. Parts on a cheaper skate may break while you're skating, leaving you open to injury. A better-made skate will also make your ride much smoother and more enjoyable.

Ask the salesperson: Is the heel brake replaceable? Your brake will wear down, and you'll need to replace it. it's certainly more practical to be able to replace a brake rather than the whole skate.

What sort of bearings does the skate use? The higher the bearing number, the smoother the ride. While an ABEC-1 bearing may be fine for you in your first months of skating, you may want a smoother ride when you get your speed up. On the other hand, there's no need to buy the most expensive skates with the highest-grade bearings if you expect to do only occasional skating.

Remember: It may take a little longer for you to save the money for the best equipment and skates you can afford, but it will be worth it. Top-of-the-line equipment will ensure many enjoyable hours of skating.

Tip: Discuss all these considerations with a parent before buying your skates and other equipment. An adult will help you make wise purchases.

Caring for Your Skates

Take the time to maintain your skates.

- When you finish skating, pull the boot liner tongue back to its original position, or remove the liner from the plastic boot if it's very wet. The next time you wear your skates, you'll be glad you took a moment to do this. If you don't, the liner will wear out before its time.

- Replace the heel brake when it wears to one-half inch or less. Pay special attention to this if you will be performing downhill slaloms, because brakes can burn up in an afternoon of downhill skating.

- Rotating and replacing wheels regularly will keep you much safer on your skates. Dirt and grit may get into your wheel bearings, so these must be cleaned regularly, too.

- Read the booklet that comes with your skates. The manufacturer will give you specific instructions about skate maintenance. You can also take your skates to a shop for maintenance.

In-Line Skating Skills

Beginning Stride

For this session, choose a flat, traffic-free paved surface—preferably with grass alongside it and a bench nearby. Ask an adult for help in choosing a place. Here are some ideas:

- A park with an isolated play area, where no one is playing
- A playground at a school when no one is there
- Your church parking lot (ask for permission beforehand)
- The patio in your backyard

Don't use a path through a park. Wait until you know how to skate well before venturing onto the paths.

Always put on your safety gear before putting on your skates; do this at the bench. Rise in one smooth motion, move onto the pavement, and put your feet in the Safe-T position.

Whenever you learn a new skill, it's a good idea to review what you've already learned before going forward. Start this session by repeating the basic drills you learned in your first session.

The beginning stride builds on the V-walk, or duck walk. The duck walk helps you learn to transfer your weight from foot to foot.

This is identical to the duck walk you did in your first session. Waddle in tiny steps, right and left, right and left. Move each skate forward a few inches each time. Keep your toes pointed out and your heels as close together as possible, shifting your weight from side to side. Remember to keep your ready position while skating; your balance will be much better. If you start to roll, just coast into a relaxed ready position and resume duck walking.

Concentrate on feeling your weight shift from side to side. This motion is essential to skating.

To do a beginner's stride, start from the duck walk and push off against the inside edge of your back skate. Again, shift your weight as you do this.

Keep your strides short, shifting from side to side. Going too fast at first can make you lose your balance.

Remember: Think about keeping your knees bent and your posture upright. Don't let your upper body lean forward; this is the wrong position and will make your back ache.

Stop!

Emergency Stop

Before you go any farther, learn how to stop. You should learn how to use your heel brake as soon as you can, but here are some ways to stop right away.

In a true emergency, when you're in danger, pitch forward and slide on your wrist and knee guards. Other ways to stop:

- Step onto grass or dirt, or whatever nonrolling surface might be handy.

- Grab something if you're going slowly. (Don't grab another person!)

- If you're going slowly enough, steer your toes together.

Heel Brake

The usual way of stopping is with the heel brake on your skate. One requirement for the in-line skating merit badge is to stop on command on flat pavement, using the heel brake.

To use your heel brake, first learn the **scissors stance**. This is a position you'll use again and again in other skills. Practice first on grass or carpet.

First get a good ready stance—except with your feet parallel and no more than a few inches apart. Keeping the braking foot in place, shift your weight to the other foot. Bending your leg from the knee, slide your braking foot forward, with all four wheels still on the ground.

Tip: When you learn new positions for extending your foot, it's easy to fall, so first practice on a nonrolling surface, and pay attention to your form.

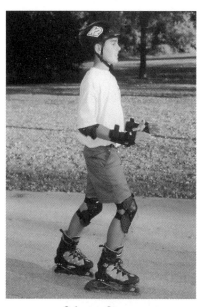

Scissors Stance

Braking Drill

Stopping is made up of three parts:

1. The approach

2. The scissors position

3. The stop

To practice stopping, you need a bit of room to coast, or approach. In this drill, you practice engaging the brake by dragging it. This helps you learn to feel and control your brake.

* Practice approaching by skating forward enough to get a good steady momentum going, then coast for at least 10 feet with your feet parallel and as close together as possible.

* Practice the scissors motion during the coast by shifting your weight to the non-braking foot while you extend your braking foot forward. Make sure to keep the feet flat, with all four wheels of both skates on the ground. Remember to keep a good ready form with your hands waist-high.

Front view, braking

* If you have a standard heel brake, engage the brake by lifting the toe of your braking foot until you feel the brake touch the pavement. Let the brake drag lightly.

* If your brake is cuff-activated, engage the brake by pointing the toe of your braking foot forward. This presses the back of your calf into the boot. If you find this difficult, you may need to adjust the position of your brake.

Repeat this braking drill until you feel comfortable with the feel of the brake. You should be able to drag the brake for several feet.

Side view, braking

Stopping

Brake lightly as described above, then push the brake pad ahead of you. At the same time you push the brake forward, drop your hips as if you're sitting down, then *quickly* straighten back up to keep from losing your balance. Although it might sound as if there are three separate actions here, that isn't the case. This should be done in one smooth motion to keep you balanced.

Practice Stopping

Practice stopping by using lines in the pavement (if there aren't any, draw a line with chalk).

Begin skating toward the line and get to a good coasting speed. When you're a couple of feet away from the line, begin your stop. It will probably take some practice before you get the hang of it without going over the line.

Try stopping from a closer distance, or when skating faster, until you know what it takes to stop at different speeds.

A-Frame Turn

In this turn, you'll turn to the left. As always, practice first on the grass or carpet.

Get into the A-frame position—a ready position, with feet slightly more than shoulder-width apart. The ready position always means your hands are waist-high.

Rotate your head, shoulders, hands, and hips toward the left. Always lead with your head, looking in the direction where you're going.

Push against the inside edge of the right skate. Let the lower body follow the upper by pushing the right skate a foot or more forward and steering toward the left.

Repeat the A-frame turn in both directions until you're comfortable with it.

Now, do the same drill on the pavement. Again, repeat the turns in both directions until you feel comfortable.

The A-frame position prepares you for the A-frame turn.

The Basic Stride

The basic stride builds on the beginning stride you learned. The difference is that you bend your knees more deeply. This lengthens your stroke and your glide, which makes you roll faster. Finally, it helps strengthen your one-footed glide, which is one of your in-line skating requirements.

Begin the session by practicing the beginning stride. For this stroke, bend your knees to take yourself closer to the pavement.

Practicing the basic stride helps a good skater get even better.

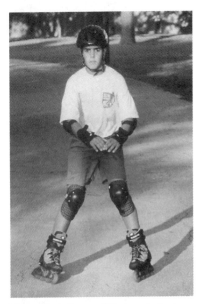

The swizzle (or scull) helps skaters get out of those tight spots.

Lengthen the duration of the glide by counting to four between strokes. This makes the stroke more efficient and strengthens your one-footed skating ability.

When you push off, don't push to the back—push directly to the side, keeping your body centered.

Recover the stroking leg fully during the glide.

The Swizzle

Use the swizzle to get around in small spaces. This skill is also called **sculling.** For your Skating merit badge in in-line skating, you are required to perform a series of linked swizzles, both forward and backward. For now, we'll learn the forward swizzle.

1. Stand with your toes out and heels touching. Push your knees together and forward a couple of inches, letting the skates tilt onto the inside edges.

2. Push outward against both heels. As your legs straighten and heels separate, you go forward. You control how fast and how far you go by the intensity you use to push.

3. Recover quickly into an A-frame ready stance (with your legs slightly wider than shoulder-distance apart).

Linking Swizzles

You can link a series of swizzles by going directly from the A-frame stance (a wide-legged ready position) into an A-stance (with the toes together). From there, move into a new V-stance and do another swizzle. Practice this until you can link several swizzles together, easily managing the changes of foot position.

Half Swizzles

1. Skate into a moderate speed and begin making forward swizzles.

2. When your toes are out and your heels are touching, shift your weight to the left skate. Begin a swizzle with the right skate by pushing the back heel wheels to the right.

3. Shift your weight onto the right skate and begin to press the left skate into a swizzle, pushing out to the side from the back two wheels. Keep both skates in contact with the ground.

    Continue practicing until you get short glides from each half swizzle.

Spin Stop

Don't try this until you can easily do the A-frame turn.

1. Skate to a moderate speed.

2. Rotate your upper body to the left to begin an A-frame turn. Make sure your A-frame stance is very wide.

3. As you put pressure on your right skate, lift the left heel and rotate the left knee out until your left heel is under your body. Both toes are now pointed outward.

4. Return the left skate to the pavement and balance your weight evenly between your thighs.

    If you can't get this the very first time—or even the second or third—just keep practicing, and you'll get it before you know it.

Snowplow Stop

Skate into a moderate speed, then begin making forward swizzles. Apply pressure to both inside edges as your toes rotate in. Increase the pressure with your hip muscles and by bending your knees. Practice this technique again and again, using a line on the pavement as a stopping place.

Parallel Turn

Don't even try the parallel turn if you're unsure of your balance. This turn requires you to lean out away from your skates, and you have to be confident you can stay on your skate edges when you do this. If it scares you, don't worry about it. Try it again later, after you have more trust in your skating.

Practice Drill

As always, first practice these moves on a stable surface—on the carpet or on the grass. You didn't know so much skating was done on the carpet, did you?

1. Start with the ready position. Move the left skate forward until the ankle is even with the right foot's big toe.

2. Put the right knee behind your left so your left thigh partially covers the inside of your upper right thigh.

3. Twist your head, shoulders, hands, and hips left and allow your knees to tip left.

4. Now straighten everything, and repeat these movements several times to get the proper feeling.

Making the Turn

Practice in a place where you have a large amount of room. Place a small obstacle (a rock, for instance) in the area where you plan to do the turn.

To do the parallel turn:

1. Skate to a moderate speed toward the area around your obstacle.

2. Put the right skate forward and lock your left knee behind the right.

3. Twist your upper body and hips halfway around to the right, and look back in that direction.

4. Let your head and shoulders pass over the right skate's outside edge into the center of the turn.

5. After you turn at least 90 degrees, straighten up.

Practice this until you can get close to your obstacle but clear it with a U-turn.

Linked Parallel Turns

1. Skate into a moderate speed.

2. Push the left skate forward and make a parallel turn to the left.

3. During the turn, push the right skate forward and move into a parallel turn to the right.

4. Continue until you begin to slow.

   Repeat until you're comfortable with the sequence.

Mobility Drills

Use mobility drills to strengthen your skating skills—especially one-footed balance. Your ability to balance on one foot should be very strong before you attempt to learn more complex skating skills, such as crossovers.

Pick-up

Skate forward into a coasting ready position. While coasting, reach down to touch your knees, then your toes, then straighten. Repeat this several times. Practice crouching down to pick up small items from the pavement as you skate. Use either hand, so you develop your sense of balance without overexercising the muscles on one side of your body.

Marching

Skate into a moderate pace. While coasting, start making short marching steps. Try to stay on the supporting skate as long as possible while the other skate is off the pavement. Work on both legs.

Single-Foot Glide

Single-Foot Glides

Skate into a moderate pace. Lift a skate up and out behind you, leaning forward slightly. Lift your arms out to the side to balance yourself, and try to hold the position as long as possible.

Training Wheel

Skate into a moderate pace. Lift your left heel and let the left front wheel bear about a third of your weight while rolling it a few inches behind your right skate. Try to keep the left skate from wobbling, and keep your knees close together.

The Kneel

Skate into a moderate pace, then do a training wheel with your right foot. Let your hips sink directly over the right heel. Divide your weight equally across the right toe and the left skate. Keep the skates as close as possible.

Crossovers

One requirement for the Skating merit badge is to perform crossovers in a figure eight pattern. The crossover lets you stroke and maintain momentum as you round corners. The crossover builds on the crab step you did at the very beginning, when you were getting comfortable on your skates. To practice the crossover, find pavement with a very slight slope.

- Assume the ready position, arms waist-high, standing with your left side toward the slope. Rotate your head and arms in that direction.

- Begin making crab steps to the left, stepping sideways and downward. After making two steps, start turning your toes toward the bottom of the slope as you return each skate to the pavement. You will begin to roll down the slope with each step.

- Maintain your upper body rotation and your stepping rhythm. Try to crab step your way around a big circle to your left.

Repeat this drill, but begin with your right side facing the slope. To get good practice doing crossover turns, find a large circle on a school or park playground. Skate toward the circle and repeat the moves you did in the session above.

Remember: Spend twice as much time practicing the direction that seems weaker for you.

Crossover—the ready position

Crab steps—sideways and downward

Backward Skating

Be sure to use a clear practice area without any traffic, since you won't be able to see where you're going.

Backward Turns

On a very slight incline, face away from the incline and assume a wide A-frame stance. Allow your skates to start rolling backward. Look over your right shoulder and sweep your right hand around behind you at shoulder height until it points down the hill. The pressure of the rotation on your right skate's inside edge results in a turn toward the right. Repeat this two or three times, starting from the top of the slope each time. Practice on both sides.

Backward Swizzle

The backward swizzle is an essential part of skating backward, as well as being a requirement for your merit badge. To do the backward swizzle:

1. Assume the A-Stance on the pavement.

2. Push outward quickly against both skates' toe wheels.

3. Recover into a wide ready position.

To link several swizzles together, pull your heels together and stand tall as you recover. Immediately turn into a new A-stance and repeat the same movements described above.

Backward Strokes

Begin a series of backward swizzles and get into the swizzle rhythm. When you reach the A-stance, shift most of your weight to the left skate. Press the inside edge of the right skate to begin a half swizzle. Immediately shift your weight to the right foot and press the left skate into a half swizzle. You should get a short glide from each backward half swizzle.

Lunge Turns

Your counselor will choose an object for you to perform a lunge turn around it. First practice the lunge turn movements.

1. Assume the ready position with your feet in the Safe-T and your hands at waist height.

2. Rotate your body so your chest is pointed in the same direction as your left toe.

3. Lunge on the right leg by pushing against the right skate's inner edges.

   Repeat several times in both directions, making sure to bring your upper body forward over the knee with each lunge.

Lunge Turn from an A-Frame

1. Skate into a moderate speed.

2. Turn your upper body to the left to begin an A-frame turn. Push the left skate ahead and position your chest over the knee.

3. After the turn, return to a normal, shoulder-width stance.

   Repeat until you're comfortable with these motions.

Lunge Turn on the Course

1. Mark out a place on the pavement to represent a turn.

2. From 25 feet away, approach the "corner" aggressively with well-bent knees.

3. About a yard before the mark, push the left skate forward and turn your upper body toward the direction of the turn.

4. Sink into a low lunge, centering your chest over the left knee and transferring your weight to that skate. The other leg has only enough weight to maintain some pressure.

5. Let both skates tip onto their left edges and press into the turn.

6. Close the gap between the skates and straighten to resume forward momentum.

   Remember to practice the turns in both directions.

Slalom Turns

Be sure you've mastered parallel turns before you attempt slalom turns, because they're closely related.

First, practice the motions used in slalom turns:

1. Start from the ready stance. Push the left skate forward until the ankle is even with the toes on the right foot.

2. Sink slightly while tipping both skates onto their left wheel edges.

3. Bring the left foot back under your hips and push the right foot forward.

4. Sink slightly while tipping both skates onto their right wheel edges.

   Repeat several times to get the feel of the slalom.

Slalom Skating

For in-line skating, this merit badge requires you to perform a series of one-footed slaloms on a gentle slope.

1. Skate into a moderate speed.

2. Push the left skate forward, sink and bend both knees to the left. This causes you to turn. As the turn progresses, your weight transfers to the right skate.

3. Rise and straighten your bent knees so you can shift your weight to the left skate.

4. As your skates straighten out from the left turn, push the right foot forward to prepare for a right turn.

5. Sink as you roll both skates onto their uphill edges, beginning the next turn.

One-Footed Slalom

   Continue practicing to refine your slalom skills.

The Power Stride

Aerodynamics is the way the wind works with (or against) a moving object. You see aerodynamic designs at work on sports cars. Automobile manufacturers try to keep their designs for these cars as flat as possible. Tall, boxy cars generally won't move as fast because their design works against the wind—causing what's known as wind resistance.

The power stride takes aerodynamics into consideration, helping you design your body into a sleeker, flatter shape that moves more smoothly and quickly in the wind. This increases your stride—and your speed.

In learning the power stride, you'll learn the tuck, the arm swing, the stride angle, and outside edging.

The Aerodynamic Tuck

This stance puts you in a position to skate fast and smooth. Practice the stance until you're completely comfortable with it. If you have a tough time balancing with both hands behind your back, try it at first with just one hand.

1. Stand with feet shoulder-width apart. Fold your hands and place them under your chin, then bend until your elbows touch your knees.

2. Relax your ankles, knees, and hips just enough to rise to a comfortable position. Your upper body should flex forward at the hips with your weight over your arches.

3. Clasp your hands in the small of your back.

The Arm Swing

Get into the power stride tuck. With both hands at your thighs and palms in, swing one hand forward and the other back.

The Angle

1. From the ready position, bend your knees to get your hips closer to your heels, as in the basic stride position.

2. Shift your weight to one foot and extend the other leg to the side. Look out toward your action skate and notice its position on the pavement.

3. Now, assume the tuck. Again, shift your weight to one skate and extend the other out to the side. Notice how much farther out the skate is. The lower position of your body allows you to add length to your stride through the length of your leg.

   Imagine a line crossing under your skates, left to right, and do your best to stride as if the line is always there, with strides going to the side.

The Edge

Now, picture a line running between your skates, front to back. The first two strides you learned kept each skate on its own side of this center line. With the power stride, you're crouched into a lower position, swinging your arms front to back, and striding straight out to the side.

You're also making this stride even more aggressive by recovering on the opposite side of the center line. This puts your skate on its outside edge, and you have to let the edge roll back onto the inside edge to push out of the stroke. This squeezes even more length out of the stride.

Outside Edge Swizzle

1. Begin by performing several swizzles.

2. As your feet close into the A-stance with your toes in and heels out, let your ankles relax so your skates tip onto their outside edges.

3. After several swizzles from your normal position, do the same from the tuck.

4. Begin doing swizzles with the right foot. Ride on the center edge of the left skate while pushing the right skate out and back to the middle.

5. Roll the right skate from the outside edge onto the inside edge as you push to the side.

   As always, practice this drill twice as much from your weaker leg.

Going Over the Line

Standing still, practice crab stepping just as you did when you first learned to skate. Now practice the same steps first from a slow coast, then a slightly faster speed. Try it in the tuck position, since this is essential to the power stride.

Practicing the Stride

Mastering the power stride requires putting four elements together:

1. The tuck

2. The arm swing

3. The stride angle

4. Outside edging

Then follow these steps.

- Begin by practicing the power stride on one skate at a time, using the basic stride for the other leg.

- In the tuck position, skate into a good rhythm, swinging your arms front to back and pushing your strides straight out to the side.

- On one skate, begin recovering on the opposite side of the center line. With the other skate, continue using the basic stride.

    Practice this again and again with the one skate until you're very comfortable with the feeling—then go on to the other skate.

Transitions

A transition is just changing directions while you're rolling. It's like a car shifting from forward to reverse.

Mohawk

For in-line skating, you are required to perform a mohawk for this merit badge. To learn how to perform this transition:

1. Skate into a good speed.

2. Begin a spin stop to the left. As soon as your left heel wheel touches the pavement, shift onto the left skate.

3. Pivot on the right toe wheel to make the skates parallel as your hips rotate backward—and begin skating backward.

Backward-to-Forward Transition

You need a slight downward slope to learn this transition.

1. Face uphill and allow yourself to start rolling backward.

2. Look over your right shoulder to begin a backward turn.

3. Rotate a quarter turn and shift your weight to the left leg.

4. Finish rotating, push off, and begin skating forward.

Backward Crossovers

First warm up with a series of crab steps to the left.

1. Begin this drill by making backward swizzles clockwise in a circle, looking over your left shoulder.

2. Transfer your weight over your left knee and continue around the circle by making the swizzling motion with just your right skate. Stretch out both arms as you bend your knees and rotate your upper body left, toward the center of the circle.

3. Push the right skate ahead of the support skate and inside the circle with each stroke. Keep your balance steady over the supporting leg.

4. Allow the left ankle to relax and tip onto the outside edge. Let your left skate go underneath your body and away from the center of the circle, passing under your hips.

Backward Crossover

5. Swizzle the right skate forward inside the circle to take your weight.

6. Push the right skate back out. Recover the left skate and return it to the pavement under your left hip.

Remember to keep your knees well-bent and your upper body rotated.

Hazards in the City

Hopping Over Obstacles

Tip: Be smart! Avoid trying to hop over anything if it's easier to just skate around it.

Any skater who plans to venture outside the backyard must learn to contend with the realities of unexpected obstacles.

Practice this stationary exercise while standing on the grass or carpet. Then practice while standing on the pavement. Be very comfortable with the stationary jump before you progress to the rolling jump. Assume a ready position, hands waist-high. Jump an inch or two off the ground. Remember to keep the ready position as your legs absorb the impact when you land.

When you're ready to try your jump while rolling, pick some line or mark on the pavement to represent an obstacle. Stroke toward it, then coast into a ready position as you approach it. Jump an inch or two off the ground, letting your legs absorb the impact when you land. Keep your knees bent as you land and your arms at waist height.

Remember to work on this position as you practice this drill again and again. Work on lifting your heels closer to your hips when you jump, so you can clear taller obstacles.

Curbs

Until you learn to hop while rolling, you'll need to approach curbs more slowly. Reach the curb at a slow coast. Lean over and reach forward with both arms as you lift the action leg and clear the curb. Step onto the curb and push off against the inside wheel edges of the support leg to continue on.

Approach stepping off a curb the same way. Lean over the curb and reach forward with your arms while lifting and extending the outside skate ahead enough to clear the edge. Remember to allow enough extra clearance for the heel brake. Land on the outside edge and push off into a glide as soon as you recover the other skate.

When you've learned to hop over obstacles, approaching curbs is a snap. Just hop up, remembering to lift your heels closer to your hips. Make sure you allow for several inches of curb height.

Advanced Slaloms

Before you begin to learn downhill slaloms, you absolutely must:

• Know how to expertly operate your heel brake.

• Have excellent balance on one foot.

• Remain calm and in control at higher speeds.

Whether or not you often skate downhill, the best way to deal with a speed where you can't control yourself is to avoid it completely. *Learn to manage your speed. Never allow yourself to reach an uncontrollable speed.*

Find a gently sloping street without any traffic where you can skate 10 feet down and stop. If you can't stop after that distance, find another location. The street is too steep for you at this point. You might also try starting at the bottom. Skate partway up, then go back down the short distance—going up farther each time you find your confidence increasing.

Controlling Your Lower Body

Warm up with the slalom drills you practiced on page 83.

• Skate down the hill in slalom form, increasing the pressure on the downhill skate by bending your knees. Tuck your pelvis and drop your hips toward the downhill heel.

• Develop a rise-and-sink motion, beginning each turn with a rise and finishing the turn with a sink. Remember your ready position throughout.

• Keep your turns shorter for steeper hills.

Controlling Your Upper Body

The position of your upper body determines whether your slaloms are effective, stable, and balanced. Learn to control this, and your slalom skating will be far more enjoyable.

• From a ready position, round out your elbows at least six inches away from your waist.

• Arch your back and tuck your pelvis and shoulders forward. Always keep your upper body curved.

• Squeeze your shoulder blades together tightly, then relax them and watch what this does to the position of your hands. Learn to extend your arm from the wrist, not by bending forward.

Tip: As you are doing slalom turns down a hill, point across your path with a finger of your opposite hand (your right hand when you're turning left, for example). As you begin to make a turn the other way, point with your other hand.

Glossary of Skating Terms*

ABEC. Stands for Annular Bearing Engineering Council, which developed a scale that measures and rates the precision of ball bearings. The scale includes ABEC-1 (the least precise), ABEC-3, ABEC-5, and ABEC-7 (the most precise).

aggressive. This style of skating emphasizes stunts, either on street courses or special ramps and pipes built for this purpose.

aim. The starting direction of an edge or sequence of steps.

ANSI. Stands for American National Standards Institute. This entity establishes standards for protective gear such as helmets and knee pads. Your protective equipment should be certified by ANSI or Snell (a similar body).

Axel. Short for Axel Paulsen jump, a popular advanced jump with 1½ forward rotations in the air.

axis. Imaginary line bisecting the circles of figure eights either longitudinally (long axis) or transversely (short axis).

barrier. The railing, wall, or traffic line forming the outside boundaries of the skating surface.

bearings. These metal encasements house the ball bearings that help give you a smoother ride on your skates.

brackets. The names of certain figure-skating turns performed on one foot.

bunny hop. A forward-moving jump in which the skater jumps upward while gliding on one foot to land on the toe of the other foot.

change of edge. A change of curve from outside to inside or vice versa on one skate without a change of skate direction.

choctaw. A turn from forward to backward or from backward to forward during which the skater changes feet, skating form one edge on the first foot to an edge of a dissimilar character on the second foot.

counters. The names of certain figure-skating turns performed on one foot.

double. Advanced versions of certain skating jumps that involve rotation in space. For example, the loop jump involves taking off while skating backward on one foot,

*The terms described here are not necessarily authorized for BSA skating activities. Your counselor can tell you which activities are approved by the Boy Scouts of America.

making one revolution in the air, and landing on the same foot. In a double loop jump the skater will make two revolutions instead of one before landing.

durometer rating. A scale from 0A to 100A used to measure a wheel's hardness; the higher the rating, the harder the wheel. (Most wheels have a rating around 78A or 85A.)

edge. In ice skating, the long side of a skating blade which makes contact with the ice. The word is also used in figure skating to describe the mark made on the ice by the blade edge, for example, "forward outside and inside edges, backward outside and inside edges." In roller skating, a curve traced by the employed skate.

employed. In use, tracing. Reference made to the carrying skate, foot, and leg.

fakie. Used to describe any trick done backward, such as a "fakie 360" (complete backward revolution).

flat. In ice skating, the mark left on the ice when both the edges of a blade make contact with the ice, causing the skater to progress without curve. In roller skating, a straight skating direction that is without curve.

free. Not in use. Not in contact with the skating surface. Unemployed.

glide. The forward or backward movement of the blade over the ice.

hockey glide. A two-footed glide with one foot following the other in a curving arc.

inside edge. A curve wherein the inside of the foot (great-toe side) is toward the center of the curve being traced.

leading. (1) In the direction to be traced. (2) In position to control or having control of the team movement.

lean. The inclination of the body to either side of the vertical.

loops. The names of certain compulsory figures in figure skating.

lunge. A body position with the skating knee fully flexed, hips and shoulders held vertically above the skating foot, while the free leg is fully extended backward.

mohawk. A turn from forward to backward or from backward to forward during which the skater changes feet, skating from one edge on the first foot to an edge of a similar character on the second foot. Probably the most-used of the direction change movements.

opening steps. Preliminary edges to gain momentum for execution of a dance or other skating movements.

outside edge. Curve with the little-toe side of the foot toward the inside of the curve.

pivot. In ice skating, a circular skating movement in which the toe picks of one skate are used as the center while the other skate revolves around the center either forward or backward, on either inside or outside edge. In roller skating, a movement where one set of the skate's wheels is used as a center while the other slides around that point.

rise and fall. An interpretive movement where the body is raised or lowered through employed knee action to impart rhythm to the skating.

rocker. Name given to certain figure skating turns performed either forward to backward or backward to forward on one foot, from one edge to an edge of a similar character.

Snell. Your protective equipment should be certified by this foundation, which tests and certifies protective equipment, or by ANSI (see entry for ANSI).

spin. A rotating action performed on one or both feet around a spot on the skating surface. There are many spins in figure skating, some taking their names from a description of their appearance (for example, corkscrew, headless, crossfoot), others from a description of the edges and/or direction used, and others from their originators' names. Some are performed on edges, some are performed on the toe.

spiral. A body position with one leg extended as high or higher than the hip, the back arched but approximately parallel to the skating surface, and the body bent forward so that the shoulders are approximately level with the hips. This maneuver is similar to the arabesque in ballet.

stop. Maneuver which causes either one or both skates to discontinue motion. In ice skating there are a number of different stops, some performed on two feet, some on one foot. Most stops involve a skidding action with one or both blades, but in figure skating some stops are made by use of the toe picks. In roller skating, the skates are placed in the "T" position to stop.

street. Refers to freestyle skating along public thoroughfares such as streets, parking lots, sidewalks, university campuses, government buildings, and other public places. Street could refer to a type of competitive course.

three. Name given to a number of one-footed turns in figure skating, all of which leave a tracing on the ice in the shape of the number 3.

tracing. The mark left on the ice after a skate has glided over its surface. It is critically important in the evaluation of compulsory figures.

tracking. The superimposition of the employed skates tracing by the partners in a dance.

vert. Short for vertical. Describes trick skating that involves combinations of aerial jumps, flips, spins, stalls, foot grabs, and other moves using specially made ramps and pipes.

waltz. Probably the best known of the ice dances, the original Skaters' Waltz, first performed around 1900 and now referred to as the European Waltz, is only one of many ice-dancing waltzes. Ice dancing also has many tangos, foxtrots, and blues, in addition to a quickstep, rumba, polka, and others.

waltz jump. A moving jump from the forward outside edge of the takeoff blade followed by a half-rotation in the air to a landing on the backward outside edge of the other foot. The waltz jump is one of the earliest jumps to be attempted.

wheel rotation. Flipping and/or switching the positions of skate wheels to help prevent uneven wear.

Skating Resources

Books

ICE SKATING

Arnold, Richard. *Better Ice Skating*. Sportshelf, 1976.

DeLeeus, Dianne. *Figure Skating*. Atheneum, 1978.

Gutman, Dan. *Ice Skating: From Axels to Zambonis*. Viking Children's Books, 1995.

Hagen, Patricia, ed. *Figure Skating: Sharpen Your Skills*. Masters Press, 1995.

Kalb, Jonah. *The Easy Ice Skating Book*. Houghton, 1981.

Kunzle-Watson, Karin. *Ice Skating: Steps to Success*. Human Kinetics, 1995.

Morrissey, Peter, and James Young. *Figure Skating School*. Firefly Books, 1997.

Olympic Figure Skating. Ice Skating Institute of America Staff. Children's, 1979.

Olympic Speed Skating. Ice Skating Institute of America Staff. Children's, 1979.

Petkevich, John Misha. *Figure Skating: Championship Techniques*. Sports Illustrated, 1989.

Sullivan, George. *Better Ice Skating for Girls and Boys*. Dodd, 1976.

Wolter, Carlo. *Figure Skating*. Watts, 1977.

Yamaguchi, Kristi, Christy Ness, et al. *Figure Skating for Dummies*. IDG Books Worldwide, 1997.

ICE HOCKEY

Brown, Newell, Vern Stenlund, and K. Vern Stenlund. *Hockey Drills for Scoring*. Human Kinetics, 1997.

Chambers, Dave. *Complete Hockey Instruction: Skills and Strategies for Coaches and Players*. NTC/Contemporary Publishing, 1994.

———. *The Incredible Hockey Drill Book*. NTC/Contemporary Publishing, 1994.

Coombs, Charles. *Be a Winner in Ice Hockey*. Morrow, 1974.

Kalb, Jonah. *The Easy Hockey Book*. Houghton, 1977.

Lyttle, Richard B. *Basic Hockey Strategy: an Introduction for Young Players*. Doubleday, 1976.

Stenlund, Vern, K. Vern Stenlund, and Tom Webster. *Hockey Drills for Puck Control*. Human Kinetics, 1996.

Sullivan, George. *Better Ice Hockey for Boys*. Dodd, 1976.

Sullivan, George. *This is Pro Hockey*. Dodd, 1976.

Williams, Barbara. *More Power to Your Skating: A Complete Training Program for Ice Hockey Players of All Ages*. Macmillan, 1980.

ROLLER SKATING

Arnold, Richard. *Better Roller Skating: The Key to Improved Performance*. Sterling, 1977.

Cuthbertson, Tom. *Anybody's Roller Skating Book*. Ten Speed Press, 1981.

Dayney, Randy. *Winning Roller Skating: Figure and Freestyle*. Contemporary Books, 1977.

Kulper, Eileen. *Roller Skating*. Capstone, 1991.

Olney, Ross R. *Roller Skating*. Lothrop, 1979.

Sullivan, George. *Better Roller Skating for Boys and Girls*. Dodd, 1980.

Waugh, Carol Ann. *Roller Skating: the Sport of a Lifetime*. Macmillan, 1979.

Weir, LaVada. *The Roller Skating Book*. Messner, 1979.

IN-LINE SKATING

Chalmers, Aldie. *The Fantastic Book of In-line Skating*. Copper Beech Books, 1997.

Edwards, Chris, and Ray Moller. *The Young Inline Skater*. DK Publishing, 1996.

Millar, Cam. *In-Line Skating Basics*. Turtleback, 1996.

Millar, Cam. *Roller Hockey*. Sterling, 1996.

Miller, Liz. *Get Rolling*. Ragged Mountain Press, 1998.

Powell, Mark, and John Svensson. *In-Line Skating*. Human Kinetics, 1997.

Publow, Barry. *Speed on Skates*. (Both Ice and In-line speed skating.) Human Kinetics, 1998.

Rappelfeld, Joel. *The Complete In-Line Skater*. St. Martin's Press, 1996.

Werner, Doug. *In-line Skater's Start-up: A Beginner's Guide to In-Line Skating and Roller Hockey*. Tracks, 1995.

Periodicals
ICE SKATING

Skater's Edge
Box 500
Kensington, MD 20895
Phone/fax: 301-946-1971
Web address: *http://proskate.miningco.com*

   Serious beginners will find the tips and detailed instructional articles, along with step-by-step photos, helpful.

IN-LINE SKATING

Inline Magazine
2025 Pearl Street
Boulder, CO 80302
Phone: 800-877-5281
Web address: *http://www.inlinemagazine.com*

In-Line Skating
4099 McEwen, Suite 350
Dallas, TX 75244-5039
Phone: 800-397-3715
Web address: *http://sportscom.com/skater*

ROLLER SKATING

Orbit
Get Rolling
P.O. Box 1115
Danville, CA 94526
Web address: *http://www.getrolling.com/orbitToc.html*
   This newsletter provides a combination of timely skating tips, industry news, and safety ideas.

U.S. Roller Skating
USA Roller Skating
4730 South Street
Lincoln, NE 68506-0579
http://www.usacrs.com

Skating Organizations and World Wide Web Sites
ICE SKATING

Ice Skating Institute of America (Recreational skating)
355 West Dundee Road
Buffalo Grove, IL 60089-3500
Phone 708-808-SKATE
Fax 708-808-8-FAX

International Skating Union (ISU)
http://www.isu.org
   The ISU is the governing body for world speed skating, short track speed skating, figure skating, and synchronized skating.

United States Figure Skating Association (Competitive skating)
20 First Street
Colorado Springs, CO 80906
http://www.USFSA.org

ROLLER SKATING

National Museum of Roller Skating (NMRS)
http://usacrs.com/museum.htm

USA Roller Skating
4730 South Street
P.O. Box 6579
Lincoln, NE 68506-0579
http://www.usacrs.com

IN-LINE SKATING

International In-Line Skating Association (IISA)
3720 Farragut Avenue, Suite 400
Kensington, MD 20895
http://www.iisa.org

Acknowledgments

The Boy Scouts of America is grateful for the technical expertise and assistance of the following individuals and organizations in the production of the *Skating* merit badge pamphlet. Jayson "Shag" Arrington and K2 InLine Skates, Vashon, Washington (for in-line skating); Lonnie Hannah, Arlington Skatium, Arlington, Texas (for roller skating); and Cheryl Pascarelli, Dallas StarCenter, Irving, Texas (for ice skating).

Thank you to the Scouts and Scouters of Troop 800, Carrollton, Texas, for their assistance with photos for ice skating.

Thanks also to Miller Sports Inc., Rancho Cordova, California, for the use of the speed skate photo on page 27.

The BSA appreciates the work of Bureeda Bruner, Consulting Partners Inc., in writing the section on in-line skating.

Books, Movies & More

Las Vegas–Clark County LIBRARY DISTRICT
www.lvccld.org